Writing for the Legal Audience

Writing for the Legal Audience

Wayne Schiess

CAROLINA ACADEMIC PRESS
Durham, North Carolina

ISBN: 0-89089-109-5
LCCN: 2002116044

Carolina Academic Press
700 Kent Street
Durham, North Carolina 27701
Telephone (919) 489-7486
Fax (919) 493-5668
Email: cap@cap-press.com
www.cap-press.com

Printed in the United States of America

For Kimberli

Contents

Acknowledgments

I am grateful to my legal-writing colleagues at the University of Texas School of Law: Christy Nisbett, Robin Meyer, and Kamela Bridges. They are great people who are great to work with.

I thank the reviewers who read and commented on the manuscript: Carol Schiess, Andrew Schiess, Kimberli Schiess, Ann Darrington, Robin Meyer, and Beth Youngdale. The book is much better because of their thoughtful suggestions.

I express my love to my children for their support: Sarah, Cori, Anna, Davis, Noah, and Logan.

But most important, I want to thank my wife Kimberli. I would not have written this book without her; she has always had confidence in me, and she patiently supports me in all that I do.

Wayne Schiess

If you want readers to understand, you can't simply throw words at paper; you've got to aim them at someone. The main reason why so many people find legal writing unclear is that it wasn't written for them. Most legal writing isn't written for anybody at all. Most legal writing is written to get it written. There. I've done it!

—David Mellinkoff, *Legal Writing: Sense and Nonsense* 65 (West 1982).

Introduction

My goal is to improve the writing of lawyers and law students.

I don't think legal writing is always bad. Often it's good enough. But it could be much better. I believe that the best way to improve legal writing is to teach lawyers and law students to focus more carefully on the audience—those who must read what we write. Too often we lawyers and law students churn out documents in a mindless, rote fashion, without thinking much about the people who will have to read them:

- If we are writing a motion, we create a document that looks like a motion—or like all the other motions we've seen—and we do not much care whether it will be easy to read and understand.
- If we are drafting a disclaimer, we cram in all the necessary legal concepts, and we do not worry about whether the consumer will be able to understand it.
- If we are writing a letter, we make sure it sounds lawyerly, whether we are writing to a client, to opposing counsel, or to a prospective employer.

I aim to change that. Lawyers can no longer write in one style; we must adapt to the needs of our many different audiences.

That's why 11 of the 12 chapters here offer specific, practical tips for writing to eleven common legal audiences. The tips focus on everything from word choice to punctuation, from document design to organization, and on much more. To improve your legal writing and to adapt to your audiences, you can use this book in two ways:

as a general guide to better legal writing and as a reference for particular legal documents.

First, I believe that if you read it cover-to-cover you will improve your legal writing in many ways. I have tried to be as thorough and as contemporary as possible in explaining the principles of good, audience-focused legal writing. The tips are current, and I've used typical examples with before-and-after versions, including explanations of the changes.

Second, if you are in the middle of a writing project, you can turn to the chapter that focuses on the audience you are writing for. You'll find practical tips for improving the particular document you are writing.

So I invite you to take up the challenge to improve your legal writing by paying attention to the needs of the audience. Write and draft so that the audience understands—and even enjoys—what you've written.

Writing for the Legal Audience

Chapter 1

A Word about Citation

I've tried an unusual approach with the citations in this book. I hope you won't even notice. But just in case you're curious, I explain myself here.

1. I've used a new citation manual.

The citations in this book were prepared according to the *ALWD Citation Manual.*[1] This citation manual was published in 2000 by a group of legal-writing professionals, the Association of Legal Writing Directors (ALWD, pronounced "all wood"). They designed it to compete with *The Bluebook.*[2] To read about the creation of the *ALWD Citation Manual,* visit ALWD's website: <www.alwd.org>.

In the interest of full disclosure, I should say that although I am not a member of ALWD, I am on a committee that promotes the use of the *ALWD Manual* for the teaching of legal citation. I do not receive any compensation for serving on that committee or for promoting the *Manual.* I'm doing it because I believe that it is a more effective teaching and learning tool for legal citation.

The *ALWD Manual* does not present a new system of legal citation. Instead, it presents a system nearly identical to *The Bluebook*

---

1. Association of Legal Writing Directors & Darby Dickerson, *ALWD Citation Manual: A Professional System of Citation* (Aspen L. & Bus. 2000).

2. *The Bluebook: A Uniform System of Citation* (Columbia L. Rev. Assn., *et al.* eds., 17th ed. 2000).

system, but it does so in a reader-friendly, clearly-written, and well-designed text. That's the advantage of the *ALWD Manual*: the rules are easy to read and follow, the text is well organized, and it offers supplemental guidance on citation that *The Bluebook* does not.

What makes the ALWD Manual better.

The *ALWD Manual* has three features you won't find in *The Bluebook*, all of which make it a better citation guide:

Fast Formats. The *ALWD Manual* provides multiple examples for each type of authority in sections called "Fast Formats." Before each chapter of the manual that covers a type of authority (cases, constitutions, statutory codes, or local ordinances, for example), there is a Fast Formats section. In the Fast Formats section you will find several examples of how to cite that particular type of authority. The examples are much more exhaustive than the examples in *The Bluebook*.

Sidebars. This useful feature provides a simple, readable explanation of a point of legal citation. Often the sidebars clarify common errors or offer writing, formatting, or researching tips. The *ALWD Manual* has dozens of these helpful sidebars on a broad range of legal research and writing topics, like these:

- Importance of Using Pinpoint References
- The Two Uses of *Supra*
- Information about Denials of Certiorari
- Locating Ordinances on the Internet
- Identifying Student Authors
- Subject Matters of Restatements

Commitment to practitioner documents. The *ALWD Manual* directly helps practicing lawyers use citation more effectively and correctly:

- In the Introductory Material there is an excellent discussion called "How Your Word Processor May Affect Citations."
- Several Sidebars are particularly helpful to practitioners: *Distinguishing Case Names from Party Names, Referring to*

    Statutes in Text, Purpose of Attorney General Opinions, and *Understanding Paragraphs in Looseleaf Services.*

- Part 5 of the *ALWD Manual,* called "Incorporating Citations into Documents," details how to use and place citations, how to use signals, and how to use explanatory parentheticals.
- Appendix 6 contains a Legal Memorandum Example that shows how citations will look in a typical document.

These features make the *ALWD Manual* easy to teach and easy to use. As a result, students and lawyers who use the *ALWD Manual* will be more knowledgeable about citation.

What makes *ALWD Manual* citation form different.

Citation form under the *ALWD Manual* does differ—slightly—from *Bluebook* form in some minor ways, but in each way, I believe the *ALWD Manual* has a better approach. The major differences:

Same form for law review style and practitioner documents. If you are silent for a moment, you'll hear a swelling cheer going up from lawyers across the country—especially from legal-writing teachers like me. Now citations will be in the same style whether they appear in a law review or a book or a trial brief or an office memorandum.

Hooray!

The Bluebook requires two different styles or "typeface conventions" for citations depending on whether they appear in law review footnotes or in practitioner documents. This distinction has caused problems for law students and lawyers for decades. Few lawyers ever completely master the separate systems, and the two systems make *The Bluebook* itself unnecessarily complicated.

The main difference between the two *Bluebook* typeface conventions is the use of LARGE AND SMALL CAPITALS in law review footnotes, but not in practitioner documents. The *ALWD Manual* has wisely banished LARGE AND SMALL CAPITALS from its citation system. One system of legal citation no matter the type of document: it's great.

As a practical matter, the existence of parallel typeface conventions in *The Bluebook* was a relic of the time when practitioners used typewriters but law reviews were professionally printed. Typewriters can't produce LARGE AND SMALL CAPITALS (or *italics* for that matter). Thus, the two systems developed.

But we use computers and word processors now. All of us have access to the same typefaces as professional printers. And the *ALWD Manual*'s authors wisely decided to abandon the differences altogether.

Simplified abbreviation forms. The *ALWD Manual* has abandoned the "apostrophe abbreviations." As you know, when an abbreviation is created by omitting letters from within the word instead of at the end, *The Bluebook* requires you to insert an apostrophe. But the *ALWD Manual* does not:

Word	*Bluebook*	*ALWD Manual*
Association	Ass'n	Assn.
Commission	Comm'n	Commn.
International	Int'l	Intl.
National	Nat'l	Natl.

I applaud this simplification of abbreviations. It makes sense.

Publisher's name for books. The *ALWD Manual* requires you to include the publisher in the parenthetical in a book citation; *The Bluebook* does not:

Bluebook	*ALWD Manual*
Wayne Schiess, *Writing for the Legal Audience* (2003).	Wayne Schiess, *Writing for the Legal Audience* (Carolina Academic Press 2003).

Legal researchers and librarians agree that this information makes cited books easier to locate.

Uniformity for periodical forms. The *ALWD Manual* has changed the citation forms of periodicals so that there is uniformity and consistency in form. Under the *ALWD Manual*, the citation form for nonconsecutively paginated journals—what most of us call magazines—is the same as for consecutively paginated journals—what most of us call professional or scholarly publications. Under *The Bluebook*, the forms are inexplicably different:

Consecutively paginated journals (form is the same):

Bluebook	ALWD Manual
Henry Wurtz, *Derivatives Behind the Market,* 55 Duke L.J. 300 (1987).	Henry Wurtz, *Derivatives Behind the Market,* 55 Duke L.J. 300 (1987).

Nonconsecutively paginated journals (form is different):

Bluebook	ALWD Manual
Kimberli Jensen, *Financial Planning,* Newsweek Oct. 24, 1999, at 28.	Kimberli Jensen, *Financial Planning,* 135 Newsweek 28 (Oct. 24, 1999).

Why is the page number at the end in the *Bluebook* citation? I don't know. And remember that I'm only showing the citation forms for practitioner documents here. If I were to show the forms for law review footnotes too, there would be two *Bluebook* examples for each type of source.

By using the *ALWD Manual* for the citations in this book, I am indirectly endorsing it. But, since I have no interest in the financial success of the *ALWD Manual*, I'll be more direct: you ought to get a copy and use it. It's a better product.

2. I've written so that you won't need to check the citations.

My goal in preparing this book was to make the text flow and to include plenty of authority for the tips I've offered. But often, including a lot of authority means the text won't flow; instead, the reader can get bogged down in citations. That's typical of legal writing—we lawyers often insert long, hard-to-read legal citations into our text, unintentionally creating "hiccups" for our readers.

To avoid that, I put the citations into footnotes. The references are there, so you have access to the authority.

But many readers like to know what authority supports an idea or assertion, and they want to know it now, without having to consult the footnotes. To accommodate those readers, I usually included a short reference to the authority and placed the bibliographic details in the footnote. That way readers get the source information now and can look up the detailed citation later.

For example, here the reader meets a long and distracting citation (a big hiccup) after the quotation:

> It is still possible to be too informal, particularly with email:
>
>> Since E-mail is so informal, there is a tendency to write in short, staccato sentences and phrases; to keep the message in all capital letters; and generally to ignore the rules of punctuation and spacing. Appearance still counts. Treat your E-mail the same as any other professional communication.
>
> Gary Blake & Robert W. Bly, *The Elements of Technical Writing: The Essential Guide to Writing Clear, Concise Proposals, Reports, Manuals, Letters, Memos, and Other Documents in Every Technical Field* 141 (Macmillan 1993).

On the other hand, in this example, the reader learns nothing about the source of the quotation and must check the footnotes if curious about the source:

> It is still possible to be too informal, particularly with email:
>
>> Since E-mail is so informal, there is a tendency to write in short, staccato sentences and phrases; to keep the message in all capital letters; and generally to ignore the rules of punctuation and spacing. Ap-

pearance still counts. Treat your E-mail the same as
any other professional communication.[3]

But in the next example, the reader gets the authors' names and a
shortened title of the book from which the quotation was taken. Yet
the detailed bibliographic information is saved for the footnote:

> It is still possible to be too informal, particularly with email,
> as pointed out by Gary Blake and Robert W. Bly in their
> book, *The Elements of Technical Writing:*
>
>> Since E-mail is so informal, there is a tendency to
>> write in short, staccato sentences and phrases; to
>> keep the message in all capital letters; and generally
>> to ignore the rules of punctuation and spacing. Ap-
>> pearance still counts. Treat your E-mail the same as
>> any other professional communication.[4]

My goal was to provide identifiable authority throughout the text,
yet still to make the text as readable and smooth as possible.

We all know that one problematic characteristic of legal writing is
the use of authority. Authority is crucial, but citing it correctly is
often tedious and difficult. Plus, the citations make our writing
clogged and disjointed.

But we cannot avoid relying on authority, and we must cite that
authority correctly. I believe that by using the *ALWD Citation Manual,* we'll be able to cite correctly more frequently and more easily. I
also believe that despite the need to rely heavily on authority,
lawyers can provide source information unobtrusively. I hope this
book shows you how.

---

3. Gary Blake & Robert W. Bly, *The Elements of Technical Writing: The
Essential Guide to Writing Clear, Concise Proposals, Reports, Manuals, Letters, Memos, and Other Documents in Every Technical Field* 141 (Macmillan
1993).

4. *Id.*

Chapter 2

Writing to the Prospective Employer

- *Aim for perfect prose.*
- *Be concrete.*
- *Be accurate.*

Whether you're just coming out of law school or are 30 years into practice, when the opportunity or need arises to apply for a job, you want to make a good first impression. Any employer will read your written materials carefully, but legal employers are especially justified in closely scrutinizing your cover letter and résumé. After all, effective written communication is one of the most important of all legal skills.[1] So sweat over your cover letter and résumé as if they were critical documents prepared for a valuable client. They are.

1. Aim for perfect prose.

Even though your résumé is probably the most important part of your written application, your cover letter is what the prospective employer will see first. Do not assume that the employer won't read it. Because it is your first chance to make an impression, the prose in your cover letter ought to be smooth, readable, and error-free. To

---

1. Joseph Kimble, *On Legal-Writing Programs*, 2 Perspectives: Teaching Legal Research & Writing 43 (1994).

present the most polished prose you can, follow these suggestions for cover letters:

- Use impeccably correct grammar, punctuation, and spelling.
- Use direct words instead of qualifiers and intensifiers.
- Choose the right words and avoid trendy ones.

Let's put these suggestions into practice. Read the following actual cover letter, in which I have changed the name of the prospective employer. The applicant seeks an entry-level associate position.

Dear Mr. Scheiss

The opportunity to pursue an associate position with Scheiss & Associates is extremely attractive to me. The firm's reputation as an innovative and forward-thinking organization is quite admirable. I am very interested in learning more about the firm and in bringing my personal strengths to your firm.

My strong liberal arts background and extensive leadership experience has served to enhance my analytical, communication and writing abilities. Through extracurricular activities and volunteer work, I have gained valuable insight into the dynamics of working with others. Multiple internships with a major law firm gave me practical experience in combining verbal and written skills with the specific needs of the firm. A well-rounded learning experience at King's College in London also honed my analytical and communication abilities.

I am eager to attain an opportunity to extend the qualities I have to offer to Scheiss & Associates. Your consideration of my candidacy as an associate is much appreciated. I look forward to the opportunity to discuss further how my qualities are a fit with Scheiss & Associates.

Sincerely,

Now let's assess the strength of this letter on the three suggestions for polished prose.

Grammar, punctuation, and spelling.

When you have an established relationship with the recipient, she might forgive you a minor spelling mistake or a slight grammatical flaw. But in a letter asking for a job from someone you don't know, you can't afford to let anything—even a missing comma—distract the employer from the good impression you are trying to make.

You probably noticed some grammar, punctuation, and spelling mistakes in this letter. I noted these mistakes:

Text	Problem	Comment
Scheiss	Spelling; it's *i* before *e*: *Schiess.*	Ouch! You'd better not misspell the name of the person you are addressing. Triple-check it.
liberal arts background and extensive leadership experience **has** served	Verb agreement; *has* should be *have.*	Because the sentence has a dual subject, the verb must be plural.
analytical, communication and writing abilities	Serial comma; the phrase should be *analytical, communication, and writing abilities* with a comma before the *and.*	Outside legal writing, (in literature and journalism, for example), the serial comma is optional. But legal writing is a form of technical writing, so get in the habit of using the serial comma; every legal writing and technical writing book recommends it.

Any one of these problems could distract the reader from your qualifications. So edit carefully and proofread thoroughly. It may help to have another person read over the cover letter to check for errors. A fresh set of eyes will often catch the small mistakes you missed.

Strong, direct words instead of intensifiers.

Perhaps it's counterintuitive, but intensifiers—like *extremely*—tend to weaken prose, not intensify it. This letter has four intensifiers, *extremely*, *quite*, *very*, and *much*. Not only do they fail to strengthen the writing, they weary the reader because there are so many of them. If everything in the letter is *extremely* something or *very* something, the intensifying effect is soon lost.

In all four cases in this letter, the sentence is fine without the intensifier. In fact, all four sentences are more than fine; they're better if we omit the intensifier. So leave out the intensifier or choose a stronger word that doesn't need intensifying.

The right word.

It's wise to get a good dictionary and use it. But dictionaries can tell you only what a word means. If you want to know how a word ought to be *used*, you'll need a *usage* dictionary. Usage dictionaries will also teach you about grammar and style; they'll tell you what words and phrases are misused, inflated, or outdated; and they'll explain common errors and misspellings. Here are three that I recommend:

- Theodore M. Bernstein, *The Careful Writer: A Modern Guide to English Usage* (Atheneum 1965).
- H. W. Fowler, *A Dictionary of Modern English Usage* (2d ed., Ernest Gowers, ed., Oxford U. Press 1965).
- Bryan A. Garner, *A Dictionary of Modern American Usage* (Oxford U. Press 1998).

Every lawyer ought to have a usage dictionary.

The usage concerns in the original letter are minor, but both could distract the reader:

Word	Problem	Comment
dynamics	This is a trendy or "vogue word."*	If it is a vogue word, many other writers are using it. Make your letter stand out by not choosing the vogue word.
attain	Probably not the meaning the writer wants here.	*Attain* means "to gain or accomplish."** Here, the writer is asking for something, not accomplishing something. The usage is awkward.

* Bryan A. Garner, *A Dictionary of Modern Legal Usage* 301 (2d ed., Oxford U. Press 1995).

** *The Oxford Dictionary & Thesaurus* 84 (Am. ed., Oxford U. Press 1996).

A revision containing all the changes recommended in this first section appears in the next section.

2. Be concrete.

Providing specific details brings emphasis to your points, and vague generalities get lost in the reader's mind. They simply do not stand out. For example, if you want to tell the reader about the extra things you have done that set you apart, you might write:

> Through **extracurricular activities** and **volunteer work**, I have gained valuable insight...

But readers will quickly forget that vague and general statement. Or worse, it will annoy: What activities? What volunteer work? The reader does not get a picture to remember or an image to keep in mind. If you really want to emphasize the extra things you have done, you would be more successful if you wrote:

> Through **working on The Journal of Appellate Practice** and **volunteering at the law school writing clinic**, I have gained valuable insight...

This vivid sentence provides concrete details that a reader can "see." Most lawyers will know exactly what it means to work on a journal. And it's easy to picture you advising students who have come to the clinic with questions.

On the other hand, providing too much detail can bore the reader and pointlessly lengthen the text. To explain the extra things you have done, you probably would not write

> As a staffer on the Journal of Appellate Practice, I participated in 11 cite-checks in the second semester of my second year. I supervised eight more during the first semester of my third year. One of the cite-checks was novel because we needed to find a rare international treaty that one of the authors had cited....

That's tedious. So when writing to a prospective employer, be concrete about your accomplishments, be specific about your activities, and explain what you can do—without excessive detail.

Here is our cover letter again. I've corrected the errors discussed in section 1, and highlighted the vague, nonspecific phrases.

> Dear Mr. Schiess
>
> The opportunity to pursue an associate position with Schiess & Associates is attractive to me. The firm's reputation as **an innovative and forward-thinking organization** is admirable. I am interested in learning more about the firm and in bringing **my personal strengths** to your firm.
>
> My strong **liberal arts background** and **extensive leadership experience** have served to enhance my analytical, communication, and writing abilities. Through **extracurricular activities** and **volunteer work**, I have gained valuable insight into effectively working with others. Multiple internships with **a major law firm** gave me practical experience in combining verbal and written skills with **the specific needs of**

the firm. A well-rounded learning experience at King's College in London also honed my analytical and communication abilities.

I am eager for an opportunity to extend the qualities I have to offer to Schiess & Associates. Your consideration of my candidacy as an associate is appreciated. I look forward to the opportunity to discuss further how my qualities are a fit with Schiess & Associates.

Sincerely,

Now that we've highlighted the general, non-detailed statements, it really ought to strike you how weak those statements are. The thinking reader is left with many questions. Here are the most glaring general statements and the questions a reader might have:

Statement	Question
an innovative and forward-thinking organization	What is it about the firm that makes it innovative and forward-thinking?
my personal strengths	Which are?
liberal arts background	A vague statement; what field, specifically?
extensive leadership experience	What *was* that experience?
volunteer work	Of what kind?
major law firm	Which one? Now I'm wondering if there is a reason you're not naming it. A bad reason.
needs of the firm	What needs?
extracurricular activities	What were those activities? Were any of them relevant to practicing law?
well-rounded learning experience at King's College	What made it well rounded? What did you do?

This letter prompts many questions, and the reader might justifiably be annoyed when first reading it. Nothing specific is ever mentioned.

Granted, the résumé will answer some of these questions, but this writer risks having the employer move on to someone else with a more memorable cover letter. Or if there are three dozen applicants, the writer risks having this letter fade into the mass of typical, general covers.

And now that we've highlighted the general statements, we see that the writer has probably brought up too many subjects for a short cover letter. The writer would be well advised to pick two or three strengths, mention them—with specific details—and stop.

For my revision, I won't worry about length; instead, I'll offer a revision that includes details for all the general statements. For purposes of the revision, assume that Schiess & Associates is an appellate-practice boutique. Here is the revised letter:

> Dear Mr. Schiess
>
> The opportunity to pursue an associate position with Schiess & Associates is attractive to me. The firm's reputation for **producing high caliber appellate briefs** is admirable. I am interested in learning more about the firm and in bringing **my writing strengths** to your firm.
>
> My **college degree in English** and **my work as vice president of the law school student body** have served to enhance my analytical, communication, and writing abilities. Through **working on The Journal of Appellate Practice** and **volunteering at the law school writing clinic,** I have gained valuable insight into effectively working with others. Multiple internships with **Baker Botts, LLP** gave me practical experience in using verbal and written skills in **a general practice.** My semester at King's College in London, **where I wrote three seminar papers,** also honed my analytical and communication abilities.

* * *

This new letter tells us a lot about the qualifications that make the applicant a strong candidate. It is much more memorable; it's distinct from the run-of-the-mill cover letters the employer probably sees. And it invites better questions: instead of "what kind of volunteer work did you do?" the employer can ask "what writing weaknesses did you see in the students at the clinic?"

In short, it gives the reader's mind something to hold on to.

3. Be accurate and honest.

When you write to a prospective employer, you are representing yourself. Of course, when you are representing a client you must be honest in your dealings with others. The ABA Model Rules of Professional Conduct require it: "[A] lawyer shall not knowingly... make a false statement of material fact...to a third person."[2]

But what about when you are representing yourself—in the letter to a prospective employer or in your résumé? Is honesty necessary? Perhaps it could go without saying, but accuracy and honesty are required there, too. Deception in the cover letter or résumé can cost you the job and can result in bar discipline.

To drive the point home, let me share with you some real-life examples of the dishonest things lawyers have written. All these lawyers received bar discipline or were held civilly liable for fraud:

- In an application for a law-school teaching position, the lawyer wrote that he was first in his class when he was 25th, that he was Editor-in-Chief of the law review when he was merely on the editorial board, and that he was a member of the Order of the Coif when he was not.[3]
- The lawyer's résumé, sent to win a potential client, said that he had opened his practice in 1991 when it was actually 1994, that he had represented healthcare organizations when he

---

2. Model Rules of Professional Conduct 4.1(a) (ABA 1996).
3. *In re Hadzi-Antich*, 497 A.2d 1062, 1064 (D.C. Ct. App. 1985).

had not, and that he was licensed in New Jersey and Massachusetts when he was not.[4]

- The lawyer's résumé said that he had graduated from Yale when he was actually two credits short of graduation.[5]

These lawyers paid a high price for their deception and exaggeration. Learn from their mistakes; be scrupulously honest in what you write when applying for a job.

If you proofread carefully, if you strive to be concrete and specific about who you are and what you can do, and if you always tell the truth, your job application will stand out. It will interest the prospective employer. It will impress.

---

4. *Baker v. Dorfman*, 239 F.3d 415, 425 (2d Cir. 2000).
5. *In re Norwood*, 438 N.Y.S.2d 788, 788 (N.Y. App. Div. 1981).

Chapter 3

Writing to the Supervisor

- *Answer questions directly.*
- *Be succinct.*
- *Be thorough.*

This chapter is directed at lawyers who must write for a boss or supervising attorney. Its aim is to improve your ability to report on what your supervisor asked you to do and to make that report an effective decision-making tool. The most common way that lawyers report to their supervisors is in the traditional legal memorandum.

But describing how to write a complete legal memo is beyond the scope of this book. To do so would mean long explanations of how to do legal research and how to organize and present a legal analysis. Instead, I'll focus on what I believe is the most important part of the legal memo: the conclusion. The conclusion is most important because it is usually the first thing—and sometimes the only thing—your supervisor will read. And I believe that if your conclusion is well written, the rest of the memo will be better, too.

So I offer three suggestions to make your conclusions efficient, accessible, and easy to read. Those things are important because of the most universal trait of the supervisor audience: supervisors are always in a hurry. They are busy. They want good information, but they want it fast.

1. Answer questions directly.

The most important part of any memo is the conclusion — where you answer the question you were asked. It's the reason the supervisor gave you the assignment in the first place. Your supervisor is not testing your ability to state the question or recite the facts. And though your supervisor *is* going to assess your legal analysis, that analysis is worthless if you can't answer the question directly — if you can't state the conclusion well.

Answering questions directly requires you to do two things:

- Avoid delay; give the answer first, the qualifiers and reasons afterward.
- Avoid unnecessary hedging; state the answer with as much certainty as you can.

To highlight these two suggestions, let's consider a real-world example. Imagine that a lawyer was given an assignment to write a memo that answers this question:

Question Presented

In Illinois, in-house counsel who are fired may not sue their employers — who are also their clients — for retaliatory discharge. Donnette Green worked at a law firm that had one client; the client treated the lawyers like in-house counsel. She reported on a partner she suspected was overbilling the client. She was fired. Could Green's suit for retaliatory discharge survive summary judgment?

Now consider this answer to the question, which we will imagine appears directly below the Question Presented on the first page of the memo.

Conclusion

The Illinois cases of *Balla v. Gambro, Inc.*, 584 N.E.2d 104 (Ill. 1991) and *Herbster v. North American Co. for Life & Health Insurance*, 501 N.E.2d 343 (Ill. App. Ct. 1987), directly impact this issue, though these cases are ten and fourteen years old respectively. However, research has revealed that recent Illinois precedent has not displaced their holdings. Moreover, although both the precedent cases held that despite the fact that regular employees are entitled to sue for retaliatory discharge on the theory that it will provide an incentive for employees to "blow the whistle" on activities that could be harmful to the public or that are illegal, attorneys are not entitled to the same right of action. Nevertheless, under the circumstances described, a possible action by Ms. Green could well be allowed to go forward. This is because although in-house counsel have been treated by the *Balla* and *Herbster* courts as having an independent, ethical obligation to disclose harmful activity, and hence no need for the incentive provided by a retaliatory discharge cause of action, Ms. Green did not represent her employer as a lawyer, as in-house counsel do. Therefore, she is not under the same ethical obligation to disclose harmful activities, and hence deserves the incentives provided by the retaliatory discharge suit.

First of all, at 210 words it's not a quick read, is it? But we'll leave that for section two of this chapter. Now to our suggestions for answering directly.

Avoid delay.

The very first words of the conclusion ought to tell the supervisor the answer to the question. Much of what lawyers write—whether in memos, letters, or court documents—fails to give the answer first. That's a weakness you should especially avoid when writing for a supervisor. Not much will frustrate a supervisor more than trying to wade through a conclusion like our example conclusion here.

If you look at this example closely, you'll realize that the answer is buried in the middle of the paragraph. That's the worst possible place for it. The legal reader will expect it to be up front; if it's not, the next place the reader will look is at the end. If it's not there, either, you've doubly frustrated your supervisor by "hiding" the answer and by forcing the supervisor to reread in search of the answer. To avoid causing these headaches, always state a direct answer in the first sentence—preferably in the first word. And keep it short.

How?

First, phrase your question presented so that it lends itself to a *yes* or *no* answer. I realize that may not be possible for all assignments. For example, your supervisor might ask an opened-ended question, like "What does the Idaho Products Liability Act provide?" Obviously, you cannot answer that *yes* or *no*. But whenever you can, pose a yes-or-no question to set yourself up for a clear conclusion.

Second, answer with a short, direct word or phrase whenever you can. Not all legal questions can appropriately be answered *yes* or *no*, but nearly all can be answered somewhere along the following simple continuum, suggested by John Dernbach and his coauthors in their popular legal-writing text.[1]

Yes	Probably yes	Probably not	No

Our conclusion would be much better if we started with a direct answer from this continuum and moved the sentence that contains a detailed prediction to the beginning. We'll also drop the word *nevertheless* because we don't need a transition word. Here's our revised first sentence:

> **Probably yes.** Under the circumstances described, a possible action by Ms. Green could well be allowed to go forward.

* * *

This is much better. The busy supervisor has a clear answer right up front. And now that we have highlighted the answer in boldface type, let's leave it that way. It will draw the reader's attention quickly.[2]

---

1. John C. Dernbach, Richard V. Singleton, Cathleen S. Wharton, & Joan M. Ruhtenberg, *A Practical Guide to Legal Writing & Legal Method* 189 (2d ed., Fred B. Rothman 1994).

2. *See* Terri LeClercq, *Guide to Legal Writing Style* 101 (2d ed., Aspen L. & Bus. 2000).

Avoid unnecessary hedging.

Your supervisor will appreciate it if you state the answer to the question with as much legal certainty as is warranted. How much is warranted? That, of course, depends on what you find in your research. And with experience, you'll become better at predicting what a judge, an appellate panel, or a prosecutor might do.

But no mater how experienced you are, you can still do better simply by the way you phrase the answer. Usually, an answer that begins with *yes* or *no* is the best approach, as I've suggested. In general, prefer those direct answers whenever appropriate.

Often though, lawyers want to hedge the answer. After all, the answer is usually a prediction of future events, and lawyers know that almost nothing is certain, least of all the law. Besides, your supervisor wouldn't have given you the assignment if there were a simple, clear answer; so you know it's probably a close call. Rather than take a strong, yes-or-no position and be found wrong, you may try to hedge; it just feels safer to qualify the answer.

But the hedged answer is weaker and less effective as a decision-making tool for the supervisor. So qualify your answer only when you must, and don't let knee-jerk, stereotypical qualifiers creep into your writing. Common qualifying phrases and words that you should guard against are

- *it would appear that, it might be said that, it is respectfully suggested that*[3]
- *seems, apparently, maybe*[4]

Yet sometimes you must qualify the answer—an absolute *yes* or *no* will not do. In his book, *Writing to Win*, legal-writing expert Steven

---

3. Bryan A. Garner, *The Elements of Legal Style* 36 (Oxford U. Press 1991).

4. Steven D. Stark, *Writing to Win: The Legal Writer* 31–32 (Main Street Books 1999).

Stark says that when you qualify your answer, you must always explain clearly why.[5] Do not leave a qualification unexplained.

Our example conclusion fails on both accounts: it is unnecessarily qualified, and we must infer the reason for the qualification from the sentences *before* the answer. For example, consider this sentence from our conclusion:

> Under the circumstances described, a possible action by Ms. Green could well be allowed to go forward.

Here's an analysis of this sentence:

Phrase	Comment	Suggestion
under the circumstances described	It properly limits the prediction to the facts of this scenario, but is that necessary? What other scenario could the supervisor have in mind?	Omit.
a possible action by Ms. Green	Is it necessary to say that the action is *possible*? What the writer probably means is that we don't know if Ms. Green will sue. So say *if*.	if Ms. Green sues...
could well be allowed to go forward	*Could* is imprecise. Lots of things *could* happen, but will they? And *could well* is just fluff. *Allowed to go forward* is also vague. We'll fix that in part three of this chapter.	Probably.

So now the sentence would read

qual. fy: If Ms. Green sues, the suit will probably be allowed to go forward.

The very next sentence ought to explain why the answer is "probably." Here, the reason the answer is "probably" is because of the two strong precedents that have denied lawyers a right to sue for retaliatory discharge. That reason should be explained more concretely than it is and should come after the answer—or we should move the answer to the beginning. We'll do those things in part 2.

---

5. Stark, *Writing to Win* at 31–32.

2. Be succinct.

The original conclusion had 210 words. By my standards, that is not short enough. How long should a conclusion be? Let's compare the conclusion to its counterpart, the question presented (or issue statement). Contemporary guidelines for writing a question presented suggest that it ought to be 75 words or fewer.[6] Should the conclusion be much longer?

No. But you may need more room because you have to give the reasons. So let's give ourselves 100 words for a conclusion; that's a good goal, not a rigid rule. And think what that means: if the question and conclusion together are 175 words or fewer, the reader gets the question and its answer within 45 seconds—60 seconds at the most. That's worth trying for.

Our original conclusion uses big words, long sentences, and lawyerly-sounding phrases. Plus, it contains some detail that we can save for the analysis. Now that we've improved the first sentence, let's take the rest of the text, line by line, and tighten it.

Original	Comment
The Illinois cases of *Balla v. Gambro, Inc.*, 584 N.E.2d 104 (Ill. 1991) and *Herbster v. North American Co. for Life & Health Insurance*, 501 N.E.2d 343 (Ill. App. Ct. 1987),	Generally, avoid citing cases in the conclusion. Doing so adds clutter and length. The supervisor knows that the full citations will be in the analysis. Just give the answer here. If the cases are particularly important, mention them by shorthand reference.

---

6. Bryan A. Garner, *Legal Writing in Plain English* 58 (U. Chicago Press 2001).

directly impact this issue, though these cases are ten and 14 years old respectively	First, just mentioning them tells the supervisor that they "directly impact" the issue. But if you must say something, say they are important. Second, give the age of a case later, in the analysis (where the date in the parenthetical is enough), unless its age is crucial to the conclusion. If so, refer to the cases like this: "The 1991 *Balla* opinion…"
However, research has revealed that recent Illinois precedent has not displaced their holdings.	We could probably save this for the analysis; or it could be shortened to "the cases are still good law."
Moreover, although both the precedent cases held that despite the fact that regular employees are entitled to sue for retaliatory discharge on the theory that it will provide an incentive for employees to "blow the whistle" on activities that could be harmful to the public or that are illegal, attorneys are not entitled to the same right of action.	A 58-word sentence. Too long. But the reasoning provided here is important. We should tell the busy supervisor about the policy behind retaliatory discharge and why that policy doesn't apply to lawyers. Specific suggestions: Omit *moreover* or choose a shorter transition; replace *despite the fact that* with *even though*; replace *are entitled to* with *may*; replace *on the theory that* with *because*; replace *activities that could be harmful to the public or that are illegal* with *harmful or illegal activities*; rephrase *attorneys are not entitled to the same right of action* into *attorneys may not*; break the sentence into two.
This is because although in-house counsel have been treated by the *Balla* and *Herbster* courts as having an independent, ethical obligation to disclose harmful activity, and hence no need for the incentive provided by a retaliatory discharge cause of action, Ms. Green did not represent her employer as a lawyer, as in-house counsel do.	A 54-word sentence. Omit the weak opener *this is because*. Instead of *treated by the Balla and Herbster courts*, just state what the courts have held.

Therefore, she is not under the same ethical obligation to disclose harmful activities, and hence deserves the incentives provided by the retaliatory discharge suit.	This sentence is acceptable, but by now the conclusion has used three different terms for a lawsuit: *cause of action, right of action,* and *suit.* Pick one.

With these suggestions in mind, here is a revised conclusion.

Probably yes. If Ms. Green sues, the suit will probably be allowed to go forward. Two Illinois cases, *Balla* in 1991 and *Herbster* in 1987, are important here and are still good law. They held that even though regular employees may sue for retaliatory discharge because it provides an incentive to "blow the whistle" on harmful or illegal activities, attorney employees such as in-house may not sue. In-house counsel have an independent, ethical obligation to disclose harmful activity; there is no need for the incentive of a retaliatory discharge suit. But Ms. Green did not represent her employer as a lawyer, as in-house counsel do. Therefore, she is not under the same ethical obligation to disclose harmful activity and deserves the incentives provided by the retaliatory discharge suit.

That conclusion is 128 words. Not bad. But let's take out the reference to *Balla* and *Herbster,* reorder it so that the reasons follow the answer, and see how much we can improve it:

Probably yes. If Ms. Green sues, the suit will probably be allowed to go forward. Ms. Green did not represent her employer as a lawyer, as in-house counsel do. In-house counsel have an independent, ethical obligation to disclose harmful activities. They do not need the incentive of a retaliatory discharge suit, which encourages regular employees to "blow the whistle." Because Ms. Green was not representing her employer as a lawyer and was not ethically obligated to disclose the harmful activity, she deserves the incentive of the retaliatory discharge suit.

That conclusion is 89 words, gives the answer first and the reasons next, and is much more clear and succinct than the original.

3. Be thorough.

One day, when I was working as an associate at a large law firm, a senior associate I knew approached me and asked me to work on a memo. He handed me a memo that someone else had written—another associate at the firm—but I did not know who. He implied that the memo was not finished and that the analysis needed to be fleshed out and the prose polished. I got started on it right away and did not think much about it at first.

The next day, as I worked on the memo—which I thought was not very thorough—it dawned on me that I was rewriting a finished memo produced by another lawyer. The supervisor had been unhappy with the caliber of the memo, so he was having it rewritten. I got a sick feeling in my stomach. I felt bad for my unknown colleague, but I also wondered if any of my memos had been assigned to another lawyer to rewrite.

I learned from that experience, and so I offer this advice: be thorough. Research carefully, write thoughtfully, and proofread several times. Be sure that any memo you write will not need to be rewritten.

Three suggestions:

Never turn in a "draft."

No matter what the supervisor says, do not turn in something that is half done, half proofread, or half right. Realize that when supervisors tell you to turn in a "draft," they do not mean a "rough draft." As Robert White put it in his humorous book, *The Official Lawyer's Handbook*:

> [When a supervisor tells you to] "Just get me a *quick* draft," "Just *whip off* a draft," or "Just dictate a *rough* draft"... [t]he emphasized words should trigger flashing red lights in your mind.[7]

---

7. D. Robert White, *The Official Lawyer's Handbook* 109–110 (Pocket Books 1983).

Ask for more time if you must, or stay up all night, but always show your supervisor your best work.

Have a trusted colleague read your memo.

Can a junior attorney ask another attorney to read and comment on a memo draft? Yes. As with all writing, a second set of eyes will often catch the mistakes, glitches, and blunders you missed. If the person you ask to read your memo is well acquainted with the supervisor, you may also get some insight into what the supervisor looks for, likes, and dislikes.

Pay attention to what you were asked.

Did you notice that our question presented, which appeared in section one of this chapter, was set in a particular procedural posture? Specifically, it asked

> Could Green's suit for retaliatory discharge *survive summary judgment?*

Asking whether a suit can survive a summary-judgment motion is different from asking whether it can win outright or whether it can "go forward" as the original conclusion put it. What does "go forward" mean, anyway? Does it mean that the plaintiff has standing? Or that the plaintiff can survive a motion to dismiss? It's not clear.

The point is that the conclusion did not address the specific procedural posture of summary judgment at all. Glossing over the procedural posture of what you were asked may slide sometimes, but it is not "thorough." So be thorough. A careful writer pays attention to the question the supervisor asked.

What might our conclusion look like if we incorporated the summary judgment aspect?

> **Probably yes. Ms. Green's suit can probably survive a summary judgment motion. Ms. Green did not represent her**

employer as a lawyer, as in-house counsel do. In-house counsel have an independent, ethical obligation to disclose harmful activities. They do not need the incentive of a retaliatory discharge suit, which encourages regular employees to "blow the whistle." Because Ms. Green was not representing her employer as a lawyer and was not ethically obligated to disclose the harmful activity, she deserves the incentive of the retaliatory discharge suit. Because her situation is novel, her suit would probably get to the jury. (99 words.)

This conclusion should make any supervisor happy.

Remember: When you write the conclusion section of a legal memo, your relationship with your supervisor is at stake, and perhaps your career is even on the line. So be direct, be succinct, and be thorough. Your supervisor will thank you.

Chapter 4

Writing to the Email Recipient

- *Think; pause; think again; send.*
- *Don't distract with formatting.*
- *Improve your confidentiality warning.*

Email is pervasive and unavoidable. If those descriptions seem negative, they are—a little. An in-house technology lawyer told me that he considers email to be the worst thing that's ever happened to writing.

But for many lawyers, like me, it is the preferred way to communicate: messages sent when I want, messages retrieved when I want, and no awkward telephone moments. Yet email has drawbacks. Many lawyers wonder how to manage the huge amount of email they receive. Some lawyers wonder about the appropriate level of formality—are emails like phone messages, chat, or formal correspondence? And confidentiality and privacy also concern many lawyers; hence the often stuffily-worded warnings that appear at the bottom of every message.

Part of the reason email is preferred is because it is so easy. But because it is so easy, we perhaps use it less carefully than we ought to on occasion. So before we get to the three tips, here are a few general points to keep in mind when using email in the law office.

First, most people do not like to receive, or try to read, long email messages.[1] So be brief. How brief? It's hard to give a firm rule on

---

1. Gary Blake & Robert W. Bly, *The Elements of Technical Writing: The Essential Guide to Writing Clear, Concise Proposals, Reports, Manuals, Let-*

email length. I like the "no scrolling" rule: Write your email messages so that readers won't have to scroll down to read the whole message.[2] That's a tough guideline to follow because you can't predict the recipient's screen size. But at least remind yourself to keep it short.

Second, maintain the right level of professionalism. It is possible to be too informal, particularly with email, as pointed out by Gary Blake and Robert W. Bly in their book, *The Elements of Technical Writing:*

> Since E-mail is so informal, there is a tendency to write in short, staccato sentences and phrases; to keep the message in all capital letters; and generally to ignore the rules of punctuation and spacing. Appearance still counts. Treat your E-mail the same as any other professional communication.[3]

Third, if the immediacy of email pushes you to respond quickly, resist. As you'll learn in part 1 of this chapter, there are benefits to taking your time. So especially if you are angry or defensive, give yourself some time before you respond.[4] In fact, even when you're not angry, you would do well to take a little time before sending an email in your capacity as a lawyer.

1. Think; pause; think again; send.

Thinking and pausing may not seem like they have much to do with composing an email message, but I have purposefully included this "thinking" advice because email is so easy to use and overuse. I've

---

ters, Memos, and Other Documents in Every Technical Field* 141 (Macmillan 1993).

2. Kelly J. Watkins, *Leave Your Smileys at School,* 29 Student Law. 24, 26 (May 2001).

3. Blake & Bly, *The Elements of Technical Writing* at 141.

4. *Id.*

intentionally broken this stage into three steps. If you follow these three steps, your emails will be better written and better received.

Think about whether you should send an email message at all.

Perhaps much of the email volume that clogs our computers could be eliminated if we took the time to think before we sent. And if we paused, we would reduce email errors, too, according to Lynne Agress, author of *Working with Words in Business and Legal Writing*:

> The advent of email…has encouraged just about everyone to try his or her hand at writing off-the-cuff, with little or no preparation or forethought. As a result, lawyers, architects, accountants—all business people, in fact—have been given an equal opportunity to embarrass themselves.[5]

Often a real letter will be better than an email because no matter how formally worded the email message is, it will still be less formal than a hard-copy letter. If the formality and seriousness of a real letter is called for, then use it.

Maybe a phone call would be better than an email message. Do you find yourself using email to avoid phone-calling? Often, that's fine. It's one of the reasons many lawyers like email. But at least stop to think about whether a phone call might be more effective. After all, in a phone call you'll have the opportunity for a real-time exchange of information and for conversational context, something that's often lacking in a thread of email replies. As Mary A. DeVries wrote in *The Elements of Correspondence*:

> E-mail, because of its speed and because computer enthusiasts love it, is often used, or misused, for messages that should be conveyed face to face, through a personal telephone call, or in a personal handwritten message. It would

---

5. Lynne Agress, *Working with Words in Business and Legal Writing* 105 (Perseus Publishing 2002).

be inappropriate, for example, to send a message of sympathy, a congratulatory message, or a thank you note by E-mail. Certain messages require a warmer, more human touch than the cold, technical approach that electronic messaging portrays to many people.[6]

So before shooting off an email, consider all three of those options—a letter, a phone call, or a personal visit—especially in the formal context of law practice. You'll reduce email volume generally, and you'll often save yourself regret, embarrassment, and headaches.

Pause long enough to review the message and correct writing errors.

Not enough of us do this. If you use email heavily, these words, from *Get to the Point!* by writing consultant Elizabeth Danziger, will ring true:

> Spelling errors, grammar gaffes, and fuzzy logic are careening through cyberspace at an awful rate. Even people who would ordinarily revise an important letter many times think nothing of pressing "send" to "distribution" without giving their message a second glance. Then their typos and garbled ideas pop straight into the computer terminals of their increasingly impatient colleagues all over the world.[7]

So read your message before you send it. Revise it. Take just a moment to polish it, and you'll save yourself the discomfort of seeing it again—when it comes back in a reply—and noticing your own errors.

---

6. Mary A. DeVries, *The Elements of Correspondence: How to Express Yourself Clearly, Persuasively, and Eloquently in Your Personal and Business Writing* 28 (Macmillan 1994).

7. Elizabeth Danziger, *Get to the Point! Painless Advice for Writing Memos, Letters, and E-mails Your Colleagues and Clients will Understand* 221 (Three Rivers Press 2001).

But if typos and garbled ideas were the only problems, we might not get too worked up. A bigger problem—according to many practicing lawyers—is the content of the email messages. Too often, lawyers see these problems:

- Sending sensitive or confidential information that should not be sent at all.
- Sending sensitive or confidential information to a list instead of to an individual.
- Sending sensitive or confidential information to the wrong person.
- Sending mistaken or unsubstantiated information.

Once again, pausing for a moment can spare you the headache and embarrassment of making a mistake that hurts your client or displeases your boss.

Sometimes the ramifications can be dramatic: consider this incident, reported in the *New York Times* in April 2002. Someone at a major New York City law firm—a lawyer, probably—destroyed the confidentiality of the bidding process for a bankrupt client by using email carelessly. This person was sending a routine email to all the potential bidders for a bankrupt client. The identities of all these suitors were to be kept secret, but the sender inadvertently included the email addresses of all the potential bidders in the message.[8] That's why I recommend that you think and pause. Then think again.

And what about tone? Because you cannot retrieve a sent email, you ought to be careful with tone. The idea here is to avoid writing to your boss or an important client in the same way you would write to your colleague or friend. Plus, you want to be careful not to hastily include insensitive statements, private information, or embarrassing mistakes—which of course can easily be forwarded to hundreds of people. So whenever you are writing an email in your capacity as a lawyer, think of it as a letter. Ask yourself these questions:

---

8. Simon Romero & Geraldine Fabrikant, *Secret List of Potential Suitors Exposed*, New York Times, C2 (April 10, 2002).

- Is this the same tone I would use in a letter?
- Have I edited as carefully as I would a letter?
- Is the content okay to send to this person *and to anyone this person forwards to?*

Of course, when you're writing to a friend or colleague about personal matters, it's different. But when you're writing as a lawyer, think of the email message as a letter, not as a note.

Send a clear message in every part of the email.

In original messages, be specific in the subject line. Your subject line will often be the sole basis on which someone decides to read or delete your message. So describe what you are writing about as briefly as you can. Instead of "Discovery matters," write "Approaching discovery deadlines in Henderson case."[9]

Modify the subject line in reply and forwarded email messages, too. You may often be tempted to click "reply," type a short message, and send it. Likewise, you might be inclined to click "forward" and send without thinking. But remember that when you click "reply" or "forward," the subject line does not change.

Are you really writing on the same subject? Think. Then change the "subject" of the message so that it reflects what you are writing about. We've all seen email messages that are replies to replies to some original message that is long forgotten, yet the subject line still says what the original sender wrote. It can be confusing. Don't do it.

Also, erase the gobbledygook, like addresses and time-stamps, that are included at the top of a forwarded message before you forward it (unless there are evidentiary or "tracing" reasons to keep it). No one wants to see all that, and it makes you look unprofessional. Besides, your reader wants to get straight to the body of the email.[10]

---

9. Watkins, *Leave Your Smileys at School* at 25-26.
10. Danziger, *Get to the Point!* at 223.

Thinking about how your reader perceives the look of your email brings us to the second writing tip for emails.

2. Don't distract with formatting.

Format your email messages so that they look professional and are easy to read. Follow these guidelines.

Put questions up front.

If you are asking a question in the message, ask it first.[11] If the reader needs background to understand the question, then ask the question and say that the background follows, like this:

> Don,
>
> Can you prepare a reply brief in Henderson v. American Technologies?
>
> You may need some background to be able to answer that, so here it is....

If you ask the question up front, you're more likely to get an answer.

Don't use trendy figures or symbols and avoid overblown punctuation.

This means that you should not use smiley-faces or other cute figures created with keyboard characters. They may be fine for informal notes to friends, according to Kelly Watkins in her piece, *Leave Your Smileys at School*, but in a professional environment, they are not appropriate.[12]

---

11. Watkins, *Leave Your Smileys at School* at 26.
12. *Id.* at 26.

You should also avoid using e-acronyms, no matter how well known you think they are: IMHO (in my humble opinion) and LOL (laughing out loud) are out of place in professional email messages.[13]

Lastly, avoid overuse of punctuation marks like this: ??? or this: !!!.

Use short, block-style paragraphs, with double-spacing between them.

To make the email message as readable as possible, present the information in short, digestible chunks, and avoid tabbing at the beginning of paragraphs. Use block style. And because you're using the block style, separate the paragraphs with an extra "return" or down space.[14] There are two reasons for using a simple, block style.

First, text formatting often does not survive into the recipient's email program—it's simply deleted. Second, sometimes text formatting like tabs, hanging indentations, and typefaces get converted into gobbledygook or codes in the recipient's email message. Using a traditional block style will eliminate most of those problems.

For example:

Instead of looking like this:

Ms. Mandel

Since we both agree that the exact sales price will depend on the then-current market price, I suggest that we incorporate a market-price provision into the contract rather than wait for the closing date to get closer so that we can get the exact price into the contract. I have drafted market-price terms in other contracts and I know that it can work well. I have the language ready to go and would be happy to send it along for your review. That's my suggestion to resolve this small impasse. Do you have a suggestion? I'd be

---

13. *Id.*
14. *Id.* at 26, 27.

open to considering it. The other issue, of course, is that the closing date keeps getting pushed farther into July. We probably need to get together to discuss the situation and agree on a firm closing date....

Your email message should look like this:

Ms. Mandel:

1. Do you have a suggestion for resolving the price-term impasse? I have a suggestion below.

2. Can you meet me Thursday (5/22) for lunch to firm up a closing date?

Suggestion on price term:

Since we both agree that the exact sales price will depend on the then-current market price, I suggest that we incorporate a market-price provision into the contract rather than wait for the closing date to get closer so that we can get the exact price into the contract.

I have drafted market-price terms in other contracts and I know that it can work. I have the language ready to go and would be happy to send it along for your review. I'm also open to considering your suggestions.

With clean formatting and a straightforward style, email messages become not only convenient, but efficient and reader-friendly.

3. Improve your confidentiality warning.

If you work in any kind of law office, you probably have a confidentiality statement or confidentiality warning that is included as a part of every email message you send. These kinds of warnings are important. They caution the recipient about confidential information, and they give instructions for how to handle a message that has been sent to the wrong recipient. Unfortunately, these warnings mostly seem to have been written hastily and for an audience of lawyers only.

The real audience for these confidentiality warnings is much broader than lawyers. If the email message has been sent to the wrong person, there's a good chance that person is not a lawyer. In that case, it's essential that the person understand the instructions and warnings in the statement. But most of the warnings read something like this:

> Privileged/Confidential Information may be contained in this message. If you are not the addressee indicated in this message (or responsible for delivery of the message to such person), you may not copy or deliver this message to anyone. In such case, you should destroy this message and kindly notify the sender by reply email. Please advise immediately if you or your employer do not consent to Internet email for messages of this kind. Opinions, conclusions and other information in this message that do not relate to the official business of my firm shall be understood as neither given nor endorsed by it.

This statement is a bit on the long side (103 words), somewhat legalistic in tone (using words like *such* and *shall*), and contains two passive-voice constructions (*be contained* and *be understood*). All three of those attributes can cause confusion, not to mention creating an unnecessarily formal or legalistic tone.

In addition, the statement covers three different subjects:

- Warning and instructions relating to privileged and confidential information.
- Inquiry about whether email is an acceptable form of communication.
- Clarification of the effect of opinions and conclusions that do not relate to the firm's business.

If the statement is to be effective—that is, if it is to convey the information and communicate the instructions—then it needs to be shorter. I also suggest writing without any legal-sounding words and in short, declarative sentences. Plus, we must consider whether all three topics should be addressed here, and if they should, how. Here is a possible revision:

> This message may contain privileged or confidential information. If you are not the addressee (or responsible for delivery to the addressee), then do not copy or deliver this message to anyone. Instead, destroy it and notify me by reply email. If you or your employer do not wish to use email for this kind of message, please notify me by reply email. This message may contain opinions, conclusions, and other information that do not relate to the official business of my firm. If so, then my firm does not endorse them.

This is briefer and clearer. That brevity and clarity was achieved by writing active, declarative sentences and by adopting a direct and plain tone. But I think we can do more.

The third sentence, about using email for this kind of message, seems out of place in this statement. Truly, that ought to be clarified before using email to communicate with another lawyer or with a client. If it is clarified in advance, it can come out of this statement.

Also, if your email program allows you to use word-processor-type formatting, take advantage of that and use boldface type to highlight the important opening phrases. (But be aware that the recipient's email program may not duplicate the typefaces.) And break up the text into two parts corresponding to the two subjects:

> **This message may contain privileged or confidential information.** If you are not the addressee (or responsible for delivery to the addressee), then do not copy or deliver this message to anyone. Instead, destroy it and notify me by reply email.

> **This message may contain opinions, conclusions, and other information that do not relate to the official business of my firm.** If so, then my firm does not endorse them.

This is a much shorter statement (69 words) and is more likely to be read and understood by both lawyers and nonlawyers.

A Final Word.

How should we spell the new word that has been created to represent *electronic mail*? If you have been paying attention, you have noticed that I have spelled it *email*, while others quoted in this chapter have spelled it *e-mail* or even *E-mail*. Currently, most dictionaries spell the word with a hyphen—*e-mail*—and accept the lowercase *e* in place of the uppercase.[15] But one usage expert has said that the unhyphenated *email* will probably prevail in the end.[16]

I am pushing toward that end.

---

15. *The Oxford Dictionary & Thesaurus* 467 (Am. ed., Oxford U. Press 1996).

16. Bryan A. Garner, *A Dictionary of Modern American Usage* 244 (Oxford U. Press 1998).

Chapter 5

Writing to the Client

- *Avoid legalisms.*
- *Limit citations.*
- *Be colloquial.*

We all write letters to nonlawyer clients at some time. Yet what we write is often poorly targeted to that audience. A partner in a prestigious law firm recently told me that he is "appalled" at the writing style of letters that his colleagues send to clients: the tone and style are too stuffy and legalistic.

As lawyers, we need to be aware that when we write to clients, we face a dramatic shift in audience. When lawyers write to lawyers, we tend to value specificity above all. So readability and clarity often take a back seat. But when we write to nonlawyer clients, we need to be sure that the big picture gets across clearly, first.

Plus, we cannot assume that our clients have a knowledge of legal language; instead, we should use common terms. We ought not clutter our prose with ungainly legal citations; rather, we should present the necessary authority in a sensible and streamlined way. And we would be wise to avoid elevated diction or overly formal language; we should write in a way that is easy to understand.

In this chapter I address three typical characteristics of legal language that appear too often in client letters: legalisms, legal citation, and overformality. I believe that when we are writing to clients, we ought to limit all three. Doing so is a sign of professional maturity and experience. I'll quote George Bernard Shaw (who used *literature* and *literary* where I'm using *law* and *legal*):

- In law the ambition of a novice is to acquire the legal language; the struggle of the adept is to get rid of it.[1]

1. Avoid legalisms.

Legalisms are "the circumlocutions, formal words, and archaisms that characterize lawyers' speech and writing."[2] They are the lawyer's way of saying something, the musty and legal-sounding words and phrases. They are the distinctive characteristics of traditional legal-writing style.

But you ought to banish them from client letters. Simply put, do not use traditional legal-writing style when writing to clients. Instead, drop the legal words and the archaisms. In essence, try *not* to sound like a lawyer.

That's a challenging standard to meet because legalisms abound in what lawyers read and in what they normally write. Thus, many lawyers will continue to use legalistic words and phrases when writing to clients, primarily for two reasons.

First, some lawyers use legalisms to impress or intimidate the client. Under this theory, the client who is baffled by the language is the client who needs the lawyer. But the client may also resent the lawyer and look for one who can explain things clearly. I say impress the client with your knowledge of the law, with your ability to get favorable results, and with your hard work. Don't try to impress clients with legalistic language.

---

1. Quoted in John R. Trimble, *Writing With Style: Conversations on the Art of Writing* 183 (2d ed., Prentice Hall 2000).
2. Bryan A. Garner, *A Dictionary of Modern Legal Usage* 516 (2d ed., Oxford U. Press 1995).

Second, some lawyers use legalisms out of habit or reflex. This is understandable. Experienced lawyers have been at it for many years; they are often immersed in their fields, naturally and comfortably at home with the legal language. Or sometimes lawyers forget what they didn't know. That happens to teachers all the time. You teach the concept from the perspective of one with 10 or 20 years' experience, forgetting that your audience has no experience. But skilled teachers—and lawyers—adapt their writing to the audience. So when the audience is a nonlawyer client, drop the legalisms.

Here is an example of how it can be done.

Examples of legalisms.

Read this excerpt from a practitioner's letter to a new client. Typical legalisms are highlighted.

Dear Mr. Wilkins:

Enclosed please find the retainer agreement. Please sign and return **same** at your earliest convenience.

Pursuant to our conversation of December 20, 2001, I have conducted legal research on the question as to whether your arbitration claim was timely under the Texas Seed Arbitration Act. Tex. Agric. Code Ann. §64.006(a) (Vernon 2001) (the "Act"). According to Texas **common law** construing the Act, the court would apply the plain-meaning **canon of construction**, *Fitzgerald v. Advanced Spine Fixation Systems, Inc.*, 996 S.W.2d 864, 865 (Tex. 1999), and should hold that **said** claim was timely.

Unfortunately, this conclusion is not guaranteed and is subject to certain qualifications discussed **herein**. *See, e.g., Continental Cas. Ins. Co. v. Functional Restoration Assocs.*, 19 S.W.3d 393, 399 (Tex. 2000).

The boldface terms are almost exclusively "legal"; that is, only lawyers use them. These words and phrases fall into different categories: *same, pursuant to, said,* and *herein* are commonly used by lawyers, but do not have unique legal meanings; *common law* and *canon of construction* have specialized legal meanings. But you can replace all of them with common terms:

Instead of	write
same	it, the agreement
Pursuant to	As discussed in, As we agreed
common law	court cases, judicial decisions
canon of construction	rule, method of interpreting statutes
said	the, your
herein	here, in this letter

By removing the legalisms, you make the text easier for the client to understand, and you avoid sounding pompous.

2. Cut formal legal citations or simplify them greatly.

The example letter I excerpted contains three legal citations. All three use correct form.[3] All three direct the reader to the proper authority. All three state the proposition they are cited for. So what's the problem?

First, they clutter up the text. Though legal readers are used to citations and, frankly, are apt to skip over them, to the uninitiated, they are large road humps. They're too long to be ignored, and yet they are not textual sentences, so readers must slow down and try to

---

3. They are correct under either *The Bluebook: A Uniform System of Citation* (Columbia Law Review Assn. *et al.* eds., 17th ed. 2000) and Association of Legal Writing Directors & Darby Dickerson, *ALWD Citation Manual: A Professional System of Citation* (Aspen L. & Bus. 2000).

figure them out. Good client writing doesn't ask the reader to slow down and figure things out.

Second, they contain specialized information that most clients won't understand. In particular, the volume-reporter-page portion of the citation can be baffling: 996 S.W.2d 864. Certainly that means nothing to the nonlawyer client.

Third, citation signals must certainly seem strange to the client. What is *See, e.g.*? Signals are a perfect example of something that has a specialized legal meaning. Their meaning is not intuitive, but is specially defined in citation manuals. We should not expect our clients to consult a citation manual.

So rather than clog your client letters with legal citations, choose one of these options:

Option A: Omit citation to legal authority altogether.

Ask yourself these questions: How important is it for my client to know the citation to the Texas Agriculture Code? Can't I just say *Texas law* or *Texas statutes*? Does my client need to know that the case I am relying on is *Fitzgerald v. Advanced Spine Fixation Systems, Inc.*, that it is found in volume 996 of the *South Western Reporter, Second Series*, page 864, and that it was decided by the Texas Supreme Court in 1999? Besides, is my client going to know what the *South Western Reporter, Second Series* is? Or that it's abbreviated S.W.2d?

Completely omitting the citations in client letters really cleans up the text and makes the document much more readable. But some lawyers will not want to go that far. And in some situations, you *do* want the client to know the names and sources of the authority.

Option B: Put the citations in footnotes.

This technique has much the same effect as omitting the citations because now the long, baffling road humps are gone, and the client can read the text smoothly. Most clients will treat the footnotes as "legal stuff" and will ignore them, and those who want the bibliographic information can find it in the footnotes. But footnotes are a mixed blessing. Some clients will be annoyed that some information is at the bottom of the page and requires them to nod up and down to take it all in.

In court papers, footnoting citations is a growing practice among lawyers and is recommended by at least one noted expert, Bryan Garner.[4] The practice has detractors, who primarily focus on the need to consult the page-bottom to ascertain the authority.[5] But for the nonlawyer client—whose need to know the source of authority is much less than a judge's—footnoting the citations can be a good compromise.

Option C: Use a shortened form of the citation.

Rather than list the entire case name and bibliographic information, simply refer to the case in a shorthand way. Leave the details in a memo to the file.

Under Option C, our letter excerpt might look like this (with the legalisms replaced):

Dear Mr. Wilkins:

Enclosed please find the retainer agreement. Please sign and return it at your earliest convenience.

As we discussed in our conversation of December 20, 2001, I have conducted legal research on the question as to whether your arbitration claim was timely under the Texas Seed Arbitration Act. According to a Texas case called *Fitzgerald*, the court would apply the plain-meaning rule and should hold that your claim was timely.

---

4. Bryan A. Garner, *Legal Writing in Plain English: A Text With Exercises* 77–81 (U. Chicago Press 2001).

5. Richard A. Posner, *Against Footnotes*, 38 Court Review: J. Am. Judges Assn. 24 (Summer 2001).

Unfortunately, this conclusion is not guaranteed and is subject to certain qualifications discussed in this letter. For example, one qualification arises from a Texas Supreme Court case called *Continental Casualty*, decided in 2000.

This letter is cleaner and clearer, with the clogging citations removed and the legalistic tone pared down. It is much more inviting to a client than the original letter.

3. Use a colloquial tone.

By "colloquial," I do not mean slangy or substandard. The phrase "colloquial tone" means "a conversational style."[6] Of course, we should usually not write to clients in the same way we speak or carry on conversation. That is far too informal and would appear unprofessional. But we *can* write in a clear, simple, and direct way that avoids pompous, turgid prose.

Ultimately, lawyers should reduce—slightly—the level of formality when writing to clients. What is too formal and what is too informal will often be a matter of taste, but consider a few examples from our revised excerpt. I have highlighted the words and phrases that strike me as unnecessarily formal or stuffy.

Dear Mr. Wilkins:

Enclosed please find the retainer agreement. Please sign and return it **at your earliest convenience.**

As we discussed in our conversation of December 20, 2001, I have **conducted legal research** on **the question as to whether** your arbitration claim was timely under the Texas Seed Arbitration Act. According to a Texas case called *Fitzgerald*, the court would apply the plain-meaning rule and should hold that your claim was timely.

---

6. Garner, *A Dictionary of Modern Legal Usage* at 171.

Unfortunately, this conclusion is not guaranteed and is **subject to certain qualifications** discussed in this letter. For example, one qualification arises from a Texas Supreme Court case called *Continental Casualty* decided in 2000.

None of these phrases is wrong or bad; they simply elevate the formality unnecessarily. They create a distance between the writer and the reader—a distance you do not want between you and your client.

Here are some possible revisions:

Formal phrase	Comment
Enclosed please find	This phrase and its sister, *Please find enclosed*, have been criticized since 1880.* Try *Here is* or *I have enclosed.*
at your earliest convenience	Almost harmless, but stuffy; try *as soon as you can* or *when you can.*
conducted legal research	One word, *researched*, is turned into three.
the question as to whether	A common legal space filler; prefer *whether*.
Unfortunately	Perfectly correct, but long. Short transition words make your writing easier to read. Use *But*. And yes, you can start a sentence with *But*.
subject to certain qualifications	Highly formal; perhaps we should omit it or revise it in a complete reworking of the sentence. Suggestion: *there are exceptions.*

* Garner, *A Dictionary of Modern Legal Usage*, at 314.

By avoiding legalisms, limiting citations, and adopting a less formal tone, we now have a shorter, clearer, and more readily understandable letter. Here is our final revision:

Dear Mr. Wilkins:

Here is the retainer agreement. Please sign and return it as soon as you can.

As we discussed in our conversation of December 20, 2001, I have researched whether your arbitration claim was timely under the Texas Seed Arbitration Act. According to a Texas case called *Fitzgerald*, the court would apply the plain-meaning rule and should hold that your claim was timely.

But this conclusion is not guaranteed; there are some exceptions, which I discuss in this letter. For example, one exception arises from a Texas Supreme Court case called *Continental Casualty*, decided in 2000.

This version meets and probably exceeds the client-reader's expectations—a legal letter that is conversational and yet professional. This is the kind of letter that a client is likely to read and understand.

Chapter 6

Writing to Opposing Counsel

• *Don't antagonize.*
• *Be specific.*
• *Think ahead.*

Just about every lawyer has occasion to write to counsel on the other side of a matter, whether it's a loan deal, a public-utilities rate negotiation, or a lawsuit. In fact, trial lawyers probably do it so frequently that it can become mindlessly routine. But we ought to take seriously our communication with opposing counsel—especially our written communication.

After all, in a letter to opposing counsel, you reveal much of yourself: your attitude, your experience, your knowledge, your professionalism. If your letter contains typographical errors, opposing counsel might assume you are sloppy. If your letter contains comma errors, opposing counsel might think you are semi-literate. If your letter contains faulty legal citation, opposing counsel might consider you inept.

Of course, you do not want opposing counsel to think any of those things. So take care when writing to opposing counsel. The tips in this chapter will help.

But first, may I put in a pitch for civility? Try to rise above the petty insults, sarcasm, and mean-spiritedness that appear in so much legal correspondence. Did you know that the American Bar Association agrees with me? The ABA Section on Litigation has *Guidelines for Conduct* that it adopted in 1996, and they contain the following:

Lawyer's Duties to Other Counsel

1. We will practice our profession with a continuing aware-
ness that our role is to zealously advance the legitimate in-
terests of our clients. In our dealings with others we will not
reflect the ill feelings of our clients. We will treat all other
counsel, parties, and witnesses in a civil and courteous
manner, not only in court, but also in all other written and
oral communications.[1]

Here's a handy paraphrase for purposes of this chapter:

We will not reflect the ill feelings of our clients, and we will
treat all other counsel in a civil and courteous manner in
written communication.

What the ABA and I are trying to tell you is to strive for a tone that
is assertive without being offensive, firm without being mean, and
precise without being insulting. Those are the hallmarks of a professional.

Now to the three specific techniques. (Note: This chapter is designed to improve the letters lawyers write to opposing counsel in any
situation, but the suggestions are especially useful for trial practice.)

1. Don't antagonize.

When your client has a problem and feels cheated or taken advantage of, is it your instinct to put on your bulletproof vest and
prepare for war? And does your war gear include a laptop computer,
so you can fire off a nasty letter?

Sometimes your client will want a fight, and you will agree. Most
trial lawyers can provoke one. But what if your client has different

---

1. ABA, Section of Litigation Guidelines for Conduct (1996).

expectations? Or what if the fight your client wants is a bad legal move? As Steven Stark, an experienced litigator and author of *Writing to Win*, has said: "[I]t is far more difficult to de-escalate a fight than it is to escalate one."[2] So write that first letter carefully; don't unintentionally antagonize your opponent.

In a recent survey I conducted, I sent sample letters to a dozen practicing attorneys in several fields and with a broad range of experience. I asked them to comment on the letters, specifically on the tone. Their thoughts and suggestions formed the basis of my recommendations here.

To get an idea of what kind of language and tone can antagonize a lawyer, let's study two samples that I used in my survey. The first is a letter sent by a plaintiff's lawyer to a defense lawyer representing a potentially opposing party. Let me set the stage.

Plaintiff's counsel's perspective.

Your client, Adam Ristov, leased a commercial property to a fast-food franchisor. Under the lease, Ristov receives a small percentage of the restaurant's profits. In addition, Ristov says that the franchisor had promised him free home delivery of food from the restaurant. But Ristov now says that the franchisor has refused to continue home delivery. Ristov and the franchisor have discussed the subject already, but this is the first time a lawyer has gotten involved. Ristov is angry, but what he really wants is to get the home delivery started again without much conflict or cost.

And by the way, you haven't had much time to investigate the underlying details.

How will you phrase your letter? What is the proper tone to achieve your client's goals? Here is one possible "first letter," adapted

---

2. Steven D. Stark, *Writing to Win: The Legal Writer* 239 (Main Street Books 1999).

from a real letter. As you read it, ask yourself if the boldface phrases are likely to help or hurt your client's cause.

Dear Ms. Richards:

I represent Adam Ristov, who, as you know, leased a property to your client, Roger Page, in December 1998. Mr. Page **perpetrated a fraud** on Mr. Ristov in connection with the lease and in his subsequent dealings with my client. That fraud needs to be remedied; **to assure a prompt resolution, I am forwarding a copy of this letter to Mr. Page's franchisor,** BurgerTime Restaurants, Inc.

When the property was leased to Mr. Page, he made certain promises about home delivery to Mr. Ristov. I believe the **franchisor ought to know that Mr. Page created this web of lies** merely to induce Mr. Ristov to enter the lease.

As you are obviously aware, Mr. Ristov is entitled to receive a percentage of the restaurant's profits. When my client recently tried to query Mr. Page about the **rash decision** to stop all home delivery, Mr. Page guaranteed that stopping home delivery would increase profits. He thereby **tried to buy off Mr. Ristov.**

* * *

Many lawyers will find nothing wrong with this letter. In fact, about 50% of the lawyers I have spoken with think letters like this are fine. On the other hand, that means about 50% object to letters that adopt this antagonistic tone.

I, too, assert that when viewed in context, the boldface phrases would be better revised or omitted. Here are the phrases with my comments:

Problem phrase	Comment
"perpetrated a fraud"	This phrase directly accuses the opposing counsel's client of fraud. That is a strong accusation and should not be made in the first letter you send to opposing counsel. Besides, it seems premature when you haven't had much time to gather facts.

"to assure a prompt resolution, I am forwarding a copy...to Mr. Page's franchisor"	In a first letter, this is a drastic step. Sure, you might hope that you will get a better or faster response by copying the higher authority, but you are also likely to get an angrier and more defensive response.
"franchisor ought to know that Mr. Page created this web of lies"	Again, the threat of contacting the franchisor antagonizes. And the "web of lies" phrase, besides being a cliché, which you should avoid, unnecessarily characterizes the opposing party negatively. Generally, that's not wise unless you intend to antagonize opposing counsel.
"As you are obviously aware"	This phrase implies that you can read the mind of opposing counsel and that you know what she is aware of. This approach is offensive to some ("How does he know what I'm aware of?") and the tone it sets is somewhat sarcastic.
"rash decision"	Again, before you have had much time to gather facts, you risk offending unnecessarily by characterizing the opposing party's actions so negatively.
"tried to buy off Mr. Ristov"	This characterizes the opposing party's actions again; it's a fairly sordid accusation.

Now, how can you improve this letter—for the purposes of getting what your client wants? I offer the following revisions, with explanations:

Problem phrase	Revision	Explanation
"perpetrated a fraud"	*broke a promise*	In the context, this is probably a more accurate statement. Plus, it does not carry the slur of a fraud accusation, yet it still states a basis for legal action.
"to assure a prompt resolution, I am forwarding a copy...to Mr. Page's franchisor"	[omit]	In the first letter, this is better left out. You may eventually decide to contact the franchisor, but you will reduce a lot of the potential tension here if you drop this phrase.

"franchisor ought to know that Mr. Page has created this web of lies"	*Mr. Ristov relied on Mr. Page's promise of home delivery when Mr. Ristov entered the lease*	This more concretely describes what happened and omits both the antagonizing threat of reporting to the franchisor and the "web of lies" cliché.
"As you are obviously aware"	*As you may know* OR *The lease provides that*	Tone down the assertion of what opposing counsel is aware of, or just state the facts.
"rash decision"	*decision*	Avoid characterizing the decision.
"tried to buy off Mr. Ristov"	*effort to dissuade Mr. Ristov was not successful*	Again, rather than comment on the actions, describe them more objectively.

A theme emerges from these revisions: report on what happened instead of commenting on it, characterizing it, or "mind-reading" the motives behind it. This "no mind reading" approach to legal writing works well in almost any context, but especially here.

Let me emphasize again that our hypothetical client is really most concerned with peacefully getting home delivery back. He probably does not want to start nasty litigation. If your client does, then the original letter may be just fine.

As a matter of fact, in reviewing the comments of the practicing lawyers I surveyed about this letter, I learned that nearly all of them believe there is a place for the "nasty" letter. Most said that the original letter here is less harsh than others they have seen. So I want to reiterate that you may decide it is appropriate to send a letter exactly like the original. But remember to consider the audience, the goals of your client, and the reaction you might provoke.

Here is a complete revision of the letter for tone:

Dear Ms. Richards:

I represent Adam Ristov, who, as you know, leased a property to your client, Roger Page, in December 1998. Mr. Page broke a promise to Mr. Ristov in connection with the lease and in his subsequent dealings with my client. That needs to be remedied.

When the property was leased to Mr. Page, he made certain promises about home delivery to Mr. Ristov. Mr. Ristov relied on Mr. Page's promise of home delivery when Mr. Ristov entered the lease.

The lease provides that Mr. Ristov is entitled to receive a percentage of the restaurant's profits. When my client recently tried to query Mr. Page about the decision to stop all home delivery, Mr. Page guaranteed that stopping home delivery would increase profits. His effort to dissuade Mr. Ristov was not successful.

* * *

The tone here is more balanced and professional. That is what you should strive for in this kind of letter. Now let's look at the same dispute from the other side.

Defense counsel's perspective.

You have just received a letter that accuses your client of several bad acts. You are writing a response. Your client, a fast-food franchisor, generally likes to take a firm stand so as not so seem like an easy mark for the sue-happy. But your client also wants to avoid nasty litigation—the franchisor believes that he has spent too much money in the past on lawyers merely exchanging accusations.

How will you phrase the response? What is the proper tone to achieve your client's goals? Here is one possibility, responding to the original version of the plaintiff's letter we already discussed. Again, as you read it, ask yourself if the highlighted phrases are likely to help or hurt your client's cause.

Dear Mr. Anderson:

I am in receipt of your letter dated December 7, 1999, accusing Mr. Page of fraud. These are very serious allegations, and I sincerely hope that Mr. Ristov is aware of the damage such **smear tactics** can have, especially when a letter such as yours is sent to a franchisee's franchisor. To try to force Mr. Page into making imprudent business decisions by the **use of defamation** and the **obvious attempt to ruin his reputation** is unconscionable, and very possibly actionable.

Mr. Page is in the restaurant business to make a profit. Be assured that any decisions that he has made regarding the Northwest Highway location have been reasonable and are intended to increase the profitability of the restaurant. In addition, Mr. Page certainly did not guarantee increased sales; rather he simply assured your client that the restaurant would be operated in a profitable manner consistent with his high standards.

* * *

Here are my comments on the highlighted phrases:

Problem phrase	Comment
"smear tactics"	Besides being a cliché, the phrase implies that you know the opposing counsel's intentions: opposing counsel did not have a legitimate concern but was only attempting to smear your client. The phrase serves only to antagonize.
"use of defamation"	You object to your client's being accused of fraud, but you now accuse opposing counsel's client of defamation. Hope of cooperation and amicable resolution is fading.
"obvious attempt to ruin his reputation"	Again, you are reading the mind of opposing counsel and concluding that his intentions are bad. And use care anytime you write that something is "obvious." That word is fast becoming a cliché, too.
"Mr. Page is in the restaurant business to make a profit."	This may sound harmless at first, but if you think about it, you will realize that it is condescending. It implies that the opposing counsel is so stupid as to be unaware that business people seek profit.

To improve this letter, I offer the following revisions:

Problem phrase	Revision	Explanation
"smear tactics"	*a fraud accusation*	This reports what opposing counsel did without the potentially antagonizing commentary.
"use of defamation"	*telling his franchisor that he is committing fraud*	Again, this reports what opposing counsel did without accusing him of anything.
"obvious attempt to ruin his reputation"	*assailing his reputation*	Again, this revision reports what opposing counsel did without negatively commenting on it.
"Mr. Page is in...business to make a profit"	*He did not make any business decisions intended to harm your client.*	This is what the original implied, but the tone here is direct and not condescending.

Here is a revision of the letter for tone:

Dear Mr. Anderson:

I am in receipt of your letter dated December 7, 1999, accusing Mr. Page of fraud. These are very serious allegations, and I sincerely hope that Mr. Ristov is aware of the damage a fraud accusation can have, especially when a letter such as yours is sent to a franchisee's franchisor. To try to force Mr. Page into making imprudent business decisions by telling his franchisor that he is committing fraud, or by assailing his reputation, is unconscionable and very possibly actionable.

Mr. Page did not make any business decisions intended to harm your client. Rather, be assured that any decisions he made regarding the Northwest Highway location have been reasonable and are intended to increase the profitability of the restaurant. In addition, Mr. Page did not guarantee increased sales; rather he simply assured your client that the restaurant would be operated in a reasonable manner consistent with his high standards.

* * *

Again, the letter is now more professional and appropriately respectful.

2. Be specific.

When writing to opposing counsel, be as specific and clear as you can within your role. You cannot reveal client confidences or release strategic information, but you can explain exactly what happened, what it means, and what you want.

For example, instead of writing, "a breach has occurred," describe the underlying facts, like this: "your client did not make the December payment, which breaches the contract." Being specific in this way will also help you as you try to avoid antagonizing. Describing something specifically will often keep you from characterizing it or commenting on it.

Plus, if the goal is to move the dispute along amicably and to resolve the dispute efficiently for your client, then specificity pays. Specific details in demand letters are easier for opposing counsel to respond to and can speed up and smooth out the resolution of disputes. Specific responses and explanations when replying to demands are also much more helpful in settling matters than are broad generalizations or vague descriptions.

What's more, if you force yourself to be specific you will be less likely to write the reflex-driven "go to war" letter that can so often provoke unnecessary delay, expense, and stress for your client.

Plaintiff's counsel's perspective.

Here is our plaintiff's letter again, with the tone revisions from section one and now with the vague and general phrases in boldface:

Dear Ms. Richards:

I represent Adam Ristov, who, as you know, leased **a property** to your client, Roger Page, in December 1998. Mr. Page broke a promise to Mr. Ristov **in connection with the lease** and in his **subsequent dealings** with my client. That needs to be **remedied.**

When the property was leased to Mr. Page, he made **certain promises about home delivery** to Mr. Ristov. Mr. Ristov relied on Mr. Page's promise of home delivery when Mr. Ristov entered the lease.

The lease provides that Mr. Ristov is entitled to receive a percentage of the restaurant's profits. When my client recently **tried to query Mr. Page about the decision** to stop all home delivery, Mr. Page guaranteed that stopping home delivery would increase profits. His effort to dissuade Mr. Ristov was not successful.

* * *

Now that I have highlighted the nonspecific words and phrases, don't they strike you more strongly as vague and general? What property? What were the subsequent dealings? How, exactly, should the problem be remedied? What were the certain promises? Finally, the "in connection with the lease" phrase and the "tried to query" phrases are unnecessarily vague.

To improve this letter, revise it so that it could stand alone— without an explanation from the author. Rather than rely on inside knowledge, which only the author and the client may have, write in a concrete, detailed way so that the letter makes sense even if someone who is not familiar with the situation reads it.

To set up a more specific letter, let's first assume that the "property" has an address. Let's assume that the "subsequent dealings" were continued promises of free home delivery. The remedy we seek is reinstatement of the home delivery. As for the "certain promises" phrase, let's assume it was just careless writing and that it refers to the same promise of home delivery. Finally, let's tighten up the language in the "query" phrase.

Our revised letter might look like this:

Dear Ms. Richards:

I represent Adam Ristov, who, as you know, leased 1285 Northwest Highway to your client, Roger Page, in December 1998. Mr. Page broke a promise to Mr. Ristov. When Mr. Ristov agreed to lease the property to Mr. Page, Page promised that the restaurant would be providing home delivery and that Mr. Ristov would get free delivery. Even later, Page reiterated those promises. But all home delivery has been stopped.

Mr. Ristov relied on Mr. Page's promise of home delivery when Mr. Ristov entered the lease. We therefore insist that home delivery be reinstated, including free delivery to Mr. Ristov.

The lease provides that Mr. Ristov is entitled to receive a percentage of the restaurant's profits. When my client recently asked Mr. Page why he stopped all home delivery, Mr. Page guaranteed that stopping home delivery would increase profits. His effort to dissuade Mr. Ristov was not successful.

* * *

There is still room for improvement, but with the revisions, the letter is much clearer and easier to understand.

Defense counsel's perspective.

From the other side, here is the letter with the nonspecific phrases highlighted:

Dear Mr. Anderson:

I am in receipt of your letter dated December 7, 1999, accusing Mr. Page of **fraud**. These are very serious allegations, and I sincerely hope that Mr. Ristov is aware of **the damage** a fraud accusation can have, especially when a letter such as yours is sent to a franchisee's franchisor. To try to force Mr. Page into **making imprudent business decisions** by telling his franchisor that he is committing fraud, or by **assailing his reputation**, is unconscionable and very possibly actionable.

Mr. Page did not make any business decisions intended to harm your client. Rather, be assured that **any decisions he made** regarding the Northwest Highway location have been reasonable and are intended to increase the profitability of the restaurant. In addition, Mr. Page did not guarantee increased sales; rather he simply assured that the restaurant would be operated in a reasonable manner consistent with his high standards.

* * *

As before, you will notice that the letter is fairly vague. What were the fraud accusations? What kind of damage could they cause? How was Mr. Page's reputation assailed? And what are these imprudent decisions he made?

Again, revise it so that it could be read alone—without the context of the letter it is responding to. Rather than rely on the content of the first letter and simply refer to it, restate the details—briefly—so that your letter makes sense even if read in isolation. Ideally, write it so that someone who has not read the first letter can still understand it.

Dear Mr. Anderson:

I am in receipt of your letter dated December 7, 1999, accusing Mr. Page of **breaking a promise about home delivery**. These are very serious allegations, and I sincerely hope that Mr. Ristov is aware that **accusing a franchisee of deceit could cause the franchisee to lose the franchise**, especially when the accusation is reported to the franchisor. To try to force Mr. Page into **continuing home delivery—when it is not profitable**—by telling his franchisor that he is dishonest is unconscionable and very possibly actionable.

Mr. Page did not make any business decisions intended to harm your client. Rather, be assured that his **decision to stop all home delivery at the Northwest Highway location** was reasonable and was intended to increase the profitability of the restaurant. In addition, Mr. Page did not guarantee increased sales; rather he simply assured that the restaurant would be operated in a reasonable manner consistent with his high standards.

* * *

Thus, an evenhanded tone and careful, specific writing can improve any letter directed to opposing counsel. But tone and specificity are not enough; foresight is vital.

3. Think ahead.

An experienced litigator once gave me this advice, which I think is valuable enough to highlight here:

- **Whenever you write a letter to opposing counsel in litigation, treat it as though you will see it again — in court.**

A colleague put it to me this way:

- **Before you send any letter, imagine it enlarged as a trial exhibit.**

Any letter? This seemed extreme. Then it happened to me.

I was representing June (names are changed) in a moderately bitter divorce against Greg. An important issue to June was the visitation arrangement for their child, Cindy. In particular, the location of pick-ups and drop-offs was becoming complicated. Greg seemed to change the place every week: first the daycare center, then the house, then a nearby restaurant.

I sent a letter to Greg's lawyer to clarify June's desire that the midweek pick-up would be at the house, and I wrote this paragraph:

> June insists that on the Wednesdays when Greg has visitation with Cindy, he pick up Cindy at 2202 Thurston Avenue. June assumes that these pick-ups will be in the range of 5:00 p.m. to 6:00 p.m.

This was just one of the dozens of letter I wrote to opposing counsel during this case. It seemed routine and safe. Besides, soon after I sent the letter, Greg's lawyer called to tell me that Greg had agreed to use the house on Thurston Avenue for all pick-ups.

But by the time we were holding depositions in preparation for a custody hearing, another concern had come up. Greg was frequently late picking up Cindy. First it was 6:15, then 6:20, then 6:30. This was frustrating to June, and she made a point of it in her deposition. In fact, she said that it was one of the reasons she opposed joint custody.

Later, at the hearing on custody, June testified about Greg's lateness at pick-ups. She had other concerns too, but she made a special point of this one. Imagine my alarm when opposing counsel rose to cross examine, and she immediately introduced my letter into evidence. "What on earth is she doing?" I wondered. Had I committed some outrageous writing error that she wanted to point out to my client and the judge?

No. She asked June to read the phrase in my letter that said "in the range of 5:00 p.m. to 6:00 p.m." She argued that the parties had agreed on a flexible range, not a rigid deadline of 6:00 p.m. My letter, in which I had focused on the *location*, had come back to bite me because I had been loose about the *time*. I had not been thinking ahead. (By the way, "in the range of" is a wordy phrase that I probably should not have used in the first place. I could have said "between.")

I had not anticipated that the opposing counsel would be dissecting every sentence, every phrase. I had read the letter as I wrote it; to me, it was about location. In hindsight, I would have been better off to have left the timing phrase out of the letter or to have been precise about my client's wishes: "Pick-up is at 6:00 p.m.—firm." We prevailed at the hearing anyway, but I never want to relive the moment when opposing counsel introduced my letter as evidence against my client.

The advice for thinking ahead when writing to opposing counsel comes down to three things, and here are some suggestions that relate to our fast-food franchise letter:

- Think ahead to future disputes, future problems, and future actions. Anticipate what might happen and write with that in mind. *Specifically, is this dispute over the stopping of home delivery going to become a lawsuit? Or is it a small matter that will go away soon? Or is this just the tip of the iceberg—are there deeper frustrations and disagreements?*
- Think ahead to the opposing client's and opposing counsel's reactions. Ask yourself what you would do if you received this letter. Write accordingly. *If there is a chance to settle this amicably, will accusing them of fraud and rash decisions make them so mad they won't back down?*
- Think ahead to the judge or jury as they hear your letter being read aloud in court. How will it sound? Will it hurt your case? Will it make you look petty, harsh, or unreasonable? *Will the judge or jury look at you as the victim, when your first letter contained some fairly nasty accusations?*

Ultimately, as you write to opposing counsel, always remember the audience. Avoid writing something that you would find provocative because it will certainly provoke the opposing lawyer. If you want to speed up and streamline the process, be as specific as you can. And always anticipate what could happen to your letter and how it could even be used against you.

Chapter 7

The Mediator

• *Write to learn.*

• *Be brief but not brief-like.*

• *Make information accessible.*

More and more lawyers must participate in alternative dispute resolution every year, and these lawyers are not just litigators. Corporate counsel, government lawyers, and even transactional lawyers will, in a typical career, participate in several disputes that are directed away from a formal trial and toward another form of dispute resolution. Mediation is the most commonly-used form.

For most mediation sessions, the lawyers must provide a mediation statement, sometimes called a premediation submission, a premediation questionnaire, or a written summary of issues. Mediators usually—but not always—require lawyers to submit these written statements before the session. Most use one of two formats: (1) the mediator may give the lawyer a set of questions—sometimes with limited space for answers, or (2) the mediator may ask for a summary of the party's view of the issues and a statement of its position. Generally, these statements are confidential and are for the mediator only. They are not submitted to opposing counsel.

No matter the required format of the mediation statement, it needs to be well written and clear. But how can it be most effective? Follow these tips.

1. Write to learn.

When the mediator requires the parties to submit a mediation statement before the session, the mediator usually has two purposes in mind.[1]

First, the mediator needs to be educated about the dispute. The mediation statement typically informs the mediator about the facts of the case and the issues involved so that the mediator will have some understanding of the case before the mediation session. Otherwise, valuable time at the session is wasted educating the mediator about the dispute.[2] Expecting the mediator to pick up the information at the session is unwise:

> The parties' time, as well as the mediator's, is better spent advocating positions and moving the discussions toward settlement than going over material for the first time that could easily have been set out in the mediation statement.[3]

Second, the mediator wants the lawyer and the lawyer's client to *learn more about their own case.* As paradoxical as this may seem, considering the first purpose of educating the mediator, it is nevertheless true. For the lawyer and the client, preparing the statement is an opportunity to begin a formal evaluation of the case that can assist them in developing settlement ranges and strategies. Thus, the mediation statement helps the lawyer and client focus on their case in a realistic and thoughtful way. According to Eric Galton, author of *Representing Clients in Mediation,* and an experienced mediator: "I want the lawyers to focus on and objectively evaluate their case prior to the session."[4]

---

1. My acknowledgments to experienced mediator John Fleming of Austin, Texas, who provided much of the background information here.

2. Eric Galton, *Representing Clients in Mediation* 55 (Am. Law. Media 1994).

3. Maryland Inst. for Continuing Prof. Educ. of Laws., Inc., *Mediation: A Handbook for Maryland Lawyers* Ch. VI (1999).

4. Galton, *Representing Clients in Mediation* at 55.

The key word here is *objectively.* The parties may have been in litigation for quite a while, and discovery may be completed, but there may have been little time for the lawyers to carefully analyze the case for purposes of settlement. To settle, you must compromise. To compromise, you must be able to see the other side. To see the other side, you must bring some objectivity to the dispute.

And there's nothing like having to write a summary of your case to force you to think about it in a clear and organized way. So when you're asked to prepare a mediation statement, set yourself to the task knowing ahead of time that the mediator may have an ulterior motive in requiring you to prepare the statement. Be aware that you are educating not only the mediator but yourself and your client.

Also, because the mediation statement is confidential and the mediator will not show it to opposing counsel, you can be candid and objective in assessing your case. As a result, you may identify weaknesses in your case that you hadn't previously discovered, and you'll be able to prepare to defend them. You'll surely identify new strengths in your case, too.

2. Be brief but not brief-like.

What an irony we have in the phrase "legal brief." Most are not. But mediation statements must be.

Nearly all lawyers are familiar with brief writing; we all probably wrote our first appellate briefs in the first year of law school. Some of us have continued to write briefs—at the trial or appellate level—for our entire careers. But the format, tone, and style of a trial or appellate brief will not be ideal for a mediation statement. You must adapt to the needs of the audience—the mediator.

What most mediators want is a simplified statement of what the parties are stuck on. But mediators, like all legal professionals, are busy. So the simplified statement must also be short. How short? Mediation expert John Fleming of Austin, Texas, says that you can accomplish the short, simple statement in "something less than 10 pages in most cases."[5] That's a challenging task, but well worth the effort because you will score points with the mediator.

In fact, if your statement is too long, you risk having the mediator skip it: Fleming points out that "Mediators, like judges, are less likely to read 70 pages than they are ten pages." So the mediation statement must be short *and* efficient. You cannot waste space. To achieve those goals, remember two things.

First, avoid formatting your mediation statement like a traditional trial or appellate brief. For example, unless the mediator requires it, do not include the standard case caption and style; instead give the names of the parties briefly:

Instead of this:

CAUSE NO. 55-5558

REGINALD E. BAKER,	§	IN THE DISTRICT COURT OF
Plaintiff,	§	
	§	
v.	§	
	§	WRIGHT COUNTY, TEXAS
STATE COMMISSION	§	
ON WAGES AND	§	
STATE LABOR	§	
COMMISSION	§	
Defendants.	§	555TH JUDICIAL DISTRICT

PLAINTIFF'S MEDIATION STATEMENT

---

5. Remarks of John Fleming to the author.

Try this:

Mediation Statement of Reginald Baker
Plaintiff in

Reginald Baker v. State Commission on Wages and State Labor Commission

pending in

Wright County, Texas, District Court #555.

Also, avoid using a table of contents (unless your mediation statement is very long, which it should not be). And do not include a table of authorities, a statement of jurisdiction, or any of the other merely procedural parts of a traditional brief. You may want to include a statement of the issues and a statement of facts, but avoid unnecessary clutter and content.

Second, avoid using the advocating tone and persuasive approach of a brief. Remember, the opposing counsel will not see the mediation statement, so there is no need to phrase everything as positively as possible or to hide all weaknesses. The mediator cannot show your submission to opposing counsel, nor is it admissible in court. So be straightforward and candid. You need not impress the mediator with your persuasive abilities, either. The mediator is not a judge, but instead "must remain neutral and never will rule on a point of law or a disputed fact."[6] As you write the statement, always keep in mind that it is "more important to educate—not to influence—the mediator."[7]

Third, do not cite legal authority in the same way you would in a brief. As noted, mediators do not make rulings or issue findings, much less enter judgments. Of course, there is no harm in pointing out the most important legal authority or a controlling appellate decision. You should. But you would be better off to attach a brief memorandum on the law, with copies of the relevant authorities.[8]

---

6. Galton, *Representing Clients in Mediation* at 55.
7. *Mediation: A Handbook for Maryland Lawyers* at Ch. VI.
8. Galton, *Representing Clients in Mediation* at 55.

Generally, avoid incorporating a detailed legal discussion into your mediation statement.

Ultimately, it is a mistake to prepare a mediation statement that looks and sounds like a brief. It is, however, a mistake many lawyers still make, according to the experts. Many lawyers unfamiliar with mediation believe that the purpose of the mediation statement is to convince the mediator that their side is correct. But to write an effective mediation statement, you'll have to let go of that impulse.

Besides, if you write a brief-like mediation statement, you send the wrong message. You indirectly tell the mediator that you did not carefully and objectively assess your own case. Instead, you wrote a persuasive brief designed to convince the mediator of the correctness of your position. Experts in mediation agree that when the statement is written to persuade the mediator, the value of the statement as a tool for case analysis by the lawyer and client is lost.[9] Since that's one reason the mediator asked for the statement in the first place, your brief-like mediation statement tells the mediator that you haven't focused on your case in an objective way.

3. Make information accessible.

We now know that the mediation statement is written partly to educate the mediator and partly to educate the author; we also know that the statement must be short and efficient. If it truly achieves those ends, it will need only one more attribute to make it superb: accessibility. In her book, *Guide to Legal Writing Style*, Terri LeClercq put it like this:

> Your readers are not going to look at your document because they have extra time or because they need entertainment. Rather, they need information—and fast.[10]

---

9. Remarks of John Fleming to the author.
10. Terri LeClercq, *Guide to Legal Writing Style* 97 (2d ed., Aspen L. & Bus. 2000).

Every important piece of information in the statement ought to be easy to find. You can accomplish that by using three techniques.

Put a summary up front.

This principle has been stressed again and again in this book, but it bears repeating because so many lawyers place the critical information in the middle. If you write an opening statement containing only preliminaries or party introductions or background facts, you're wasting space. Legal-writing expert Bryan Garner believes that "The ideal introduction concisely states the exact points at issue. Stripped of all extraneous matter, the intro serves as an executive summary: it places the essential ideas before the reader."[11]

So save the factual background for the facts section, and let the title of your document introduce the parties. In the first paragraph of your mediation statement, place the "essential ideas" before the mediator. Consider this example.

Original opening paragraph of mediation statement.

Factual Background

In June of 1997, Baker began employment with the State Commission on Wages (SCW) as Assistant Director of Administrative Services. Baker was subsequently promoted twice while at SCW. Specifically, in late June 1998, Baker was promoted to Executive Director for Finance and Administration, and in February 1999, Baker was promoted to Chief Executive and Administrative Officer for SCW. As Chief Executive and Administrative Officer, Baker received a salary of approximately $67,000.

Obviously, this paragraph tells us nothing about the crux of the dispute before the mediator. For this reason, I always advise against *opening* with factual background. Of course, you must give the fac-

---

11. Bryan A. Garner, *Legal Writing in Plain English: A Text with Exercises* 55 (U. Chicago Press 2001).

tual background somewhere, but not first. State the issue and your proposed resolution of it first, like this:

Revised opening paragraph of mediation statement.

Summary

When the State Commission on Wages was placed in con-servatorship, the conservators told Reginald Baker that they were going to eliminate the position he held as Chief Exec-utive and Administrative Officer. Evidence now shows that they did not eliminate the position. Instead, they hired an-other person, an employee of one of the conservators with less experience than Baker, as Chief Executive and Adminis-trative Officer. They fired Baker. He seeks damages for wrongful termination.

This paragraph tells the mediator the main point of the dispute and how this party views the issue. It's an efficient and effective summary.

Summarize facts into a narrative.

By the time you're writing the mediation statement, you may have completed discovery—including depositions. So you ought to know the facts well. But the mediator does not, and you must pre-sent the facts in an understandable way. In writing about the facts you have discovered, follow these tips.

Avoid telling the story in the order that you learned it. It may have come to you in bits and pieces, from depositions and docu-ments. But you must consolidate that information, organize it, and present it in a readable narrative. As much as possible, present a chronological story. Though you may occasionally abandon chrono-logical order so you can emphasize a point, varying from chrono-logical order is a technique of persuasion that is usually out of place in a mediation statement.

Stories are usually told in chronological order, and stories are memorable. As legal-writing expert Terri LeClercq put it, "Chronology's strength is its narrative; of all organizational patterns, a reader is most likely to remember a story."[13]

Also, avoid the all-too-common brief-writing practice of summarizing testimony witness-by-witness. That technique is sure to annoy mediators as much as it annoys judges: Judge Roger J. Miner, of the United States Court of Appeals for the Second Circuit, says that "Some lawyers have the bad habit of presenting the facts by summarizing the testimony of each witness. We much prefer a narrative of the facts."[14]

Design documents with white space and clear formatting.

Document design and formatting are, on the surface, simple things that might seem unimportant. Or perhaps they seem beneath us as attorneys. Yet recognized experts in legal writing continue to tell us that it matters how our documents look:

- "Failing to use these [document design] options knowledgeably puts the writer at a disadvantage because most readers have become accustomed to well-designed documents." — Bryan Garner, in *A Dictionary of Modern Legal Usage.*[15]
- "Modern law offices…are no longer confined to preprinted forms and typewritten documents.…[L]egal writers now face decisions about formatting virtually every piece of writing produced." — Martha Faulk and Irving Mehler in *The Elements of Legal Writing.*[16]

---

13. Terri LeClercq, *Expert Legal Writing* 104 (U. Tex. Press 1995).

14. Roger J. Miner, *Twenty-Five "Dos" for Appellate Brief Writers*, 3 Scribes J. Leg. Writing 19, 22 (1992).

15. Bryan A. Garner, *A Dictionary of Modern Legal Usage* 290 (2d ed., Oxford U. Press 1995).

16. Martha Faulk & Irving Mehler, *The Elements of Legal Writing: A Guide to the Principles of Writing Clear, Concise, and Persuasive Legal Documents* 99 (Macmillan 1994).

- "[G]ood document design can encourage readers and make them more efficient in extracting information from a document.... Legal writers who want to give their writing the best chance of being read and understood will pay attention to document design."—Michéle Asprey in *Plain Language for Lawyers*.[17]

And in *Guide to Legal Writing Style*, Terri LeClercq includes a chapter called "Formatting for a Visual Society," in which she instructs lawyers to "[create] pages that are visually inviting, logically organized, and understandable on the first reading."[18]

For mediation statements, you can use three contemporary techniques for designing a reader-friendly document.

(a) *White space.* Leave ample space between the sections or parts of the statement. This does not mean that you must always double-space the text. In fact, if you use ample white space and short paragraphs, single-spaced text will look better and be easier to read. Follow the requirements of the mediator, though. And make sure that the margins are at least one inch.

(b) *Type.* Select a readable type size, probably 12- or 13-point type if you're using Times New Roman. Never submit a mediation statement in 11-point type or smaller. And use a larger type size to make headings stand out. In Times New Roman, I suggest 13-point type for the text and 14-point type for headings. But remember moderation and professionalism. Don't get carried away with fancy typefaces or excessive size variations.

(c) *Graphics.* Use hanging indentations to set off important information. Use bullets to highlight the content of lists. Use text boxes or tables to draw attention to critical information or to make a summary stand out.

---

17. Michéle M. Asprey, *Plain Language for Lawyers* 204 (2d ed., Federation Press 1996).

18. LeClercq, *Guide to Legal Writing Style* at 98.

In the following excerpt, notice the use of type sizes, boldface text, bullets, and a text box.

[heading omitted]

Summary

When the State Commission on Wages was placed in conservatorship, the conservators told Reginald Baker that they were going to eliminate his position—Chief Executive and Administrative Officer. Evidence now shows that they did not eliminate the position. Instead, they hired an employee of one of the conservators—with less experience than Baker—as Chief Executive and Administrative Officer. They fired Baker. He seeks damages for wrongful termination.

Facts

Reginald Baker is an experienced administrative-agency supervisor with impressive credentials:

- He has a B.S. in municipal engineering from Texas A&M University.
- He has a Master of Public Administration from Louisiana State University.
- He has worked for state agencies for 14 years, with seven years of supervisory experience.

Baker began working at the State Commission on Wages in 1997 as Assistant Director of Administrative Services. He was twice promoted while at the Commission, first to Executive Director for Finance and Administration, and in February 1999 to Chief Executive and Administrative Officer. His salary was $67,000....

The Commission was placed in conservatorship in 2000. The parties do not dispute that Mr. Baker was not at fault for the causes of the Commission going into conservatorship....

The conservators hired Rita Harrow as the new Chief Executive and Administrative Officer; she holds a Bachelor of Industrial and Labor Relations from Cornell University and a Masters of Public Administration from the University of Alabama. We acknowledge that her education suits her for the work of Chief Executive and Administrative Officer. But she had not previously worked in a supervisory position at a state agency. She was employed at Hardy Technology Systems, owned by one of the conservators, Jake Hardy....

Proposed Dispute Resolution

Mr. Baker believes that the conservators hired a business associate of one of the conservators to replace him but deceived him as to that fact. Their actions caused him to be unemployed for nearly two years and to miss out on career-advancement opportunities. He specifically seeks the following redress:

> 1. $125,000 in monetary damages.
> 2. Reinstatement in a supervisory position at the Commission.

This excerpted statement is straightforward, well formatted, and easy to read. It invites the mediator to quickly and easily grasp the key facts and the important issues. And it presents the information without exaggeration and without hiding anything.

Chapter 8

Writing to the Trial Judge

For motions

- *Use a bold synopsis.*
- *Organize overtly.*
- *Be honest.*

For affidavits

- *Use a bold synopsis.*
- *Use headings.*
- *Cut archaic, formulaic language.*

During a career, a trial lawyer will write hundreds—if not thousands—of papers directed at trial judges. Yet so much of what is written for trial judges is not well suited to that audience. Too often, we lawyers treat judges as if they were reading machines—obligated to read what we submit, no matter how difficult it is.

But trial judges, as an audience, are operating under demanding circumstances:

- Trial judges are busy, yet many court papers require them to plow through lengthy preliminaries.
- Trial judges deal with numerous matters, yet many court papers bury the critical point—what separates this case from others—in undifferentiated blocks of text.
- Trial judges must make informed decisions, yet some court papers fudge on the facts or the law or both.

This chapter can't fix all the problems with writing for trial judges, but it offers six suggestions—three for motions and three for affidavits—that will help you get the trial judge's attention, keep it, and deserve it.

For Motions

1. Use a bold synopsis.

Do you begin your court papers by introducing the parties and the procedural background? Stop it.

You're squandering a great chance to get your point across. One experienced practitioner and expert writer, Beverly Ray Burlingame, put it this way:

> By devoting the entire opening paragraph to restating the needlessly long title, lawyers waste judges' time and sacrifice a valuable chance for persuasion.[1]

So put a summary of your point or points up front. Giving a summary at the beginning is not a new idea. Many legal-writing professionals recommend it. Here's a sampling of quotations:

> Virtually all analytical or persuasive writing should have a summary on page one.— Bryan Garner, *Legal Writing in Plain English.*[2]

> State your conclusion on any specific issue at the outset.— John Dernbach, *et al., A Practical Guide to Legal Writing & Legal Method.*[3]

---

1. Beverly Ray Burlingame, *On Beginning a Court Paper,* 6 Scribes J. Leg. Writing 160, 161 (1996–1997).

2. Bryan A. Garner, *Legal Writing in Plain English: A Text with Exercises* 58 (U. Chicago Press 2001).

3. John C. Dernbach, Richard V. Singleton II, Cathleen S. Wharton & Joan M. Ruhtenberg, *A Practical Guide to Legal Writing & Legal Method* 153 (2d ed., Fred B. Rothman Publications 1994).

In each part of your legal analysis, give the bottom line first.—Irwin Alterman, *Plain & Accurate Style in Court Papers*.[4]

All briefs should have a first-page, introductory summary, whether the rules require one or not.—Steven D. Stark, *Writing to Win*.[5]

So in any court paper, put a summary right at the beginning. Whether you state the issue, summarize your position, or assert the correct result, you should do it up front. Yet too many court papers don't.

I recommend that when you submit a motion to a trial judge, you begin with a bold synopsis, an idea I wrote about in a Texas Bar Journal piece called *The Bold Synopsis: A Way to Improve Your Motions*.[6] It's an excellent way to put a summary right up front. To use it, write a one- or two-sentence summary of your point, highlight it with boldface text, and set it off with indentations. To see how it works, compare these before-and-after examples of trial motions:

Before—a typical first page.

DEFENDANTS' MOTION FOR SUMMARY JUDGMENT & BRIEF IN SUPPORT THEREOF

TO THE HONORABLE JUDGE OF SAID COURT:

COMES NOW CHRIS SMITH AND READY-FOODS, INC., D/B/A ARBY'S, collectively ("Defendants"), pursuant

---

4. Irwin Alterman, *Plain & Accurate Style in Court Papers* 97 (ALI-ABA 1987).

5. Steven D. Stark, *Writing to Win: The Legal Writer* 144 (Main Street Books 1999).

6. Wayne Schiess, *The Bold Synopsis: A Way to Improve Your Motions*, 63 Tex. B.J. 1030 (Dec. 2000).

> to Rule 166a, and move this Court to grant summary judg-
> ment against all claims of Remy Gonzalez ("Plaintiff"), in
> the above-referenced matter....

* * *

This standard opener tells the judge almost nothing about the issue and nothing specific about the grounds for the motion. It is all preliminary. Instead, get right to the point; tell the judge the purpose of the motion, specifically, right at the beginning.

After—with a bold synopsis.

Motion for Summary Judgment

> **Chris Smith and Arby's move for summary judg-
> ment because they were never the plaintiff's em-
> ployer under Texas law. In addition, the plaintiff
> has not exhausted his administrative remedies.**

> 1. Background....

* * *

Here's another before-and-after example. Notice that the writer takes up a good portion of the original opener with defining party names. If that is necessary at all, the first paragraph is not the place to do it. Get the judge focused on your points, not on the parties' defined names:

Before—a typical opener.

PLAINTIFF'S TRIAL BRIEF

> Plaintiff, Reginald E. Curtis ("Curtis"), files his Trial Brief
> in his suit against the Texas Commission on Wages
> ("TCW") and the Texas Labor Commission ("TLC") (col-
> lectively, "Defendants"), as follows...

* * *

After—with a bold synopsis.

Plaintiff's Trial Brief

The EEOC's conclusions and factual findings should be admitted into evidence here. Its hearings involved the same parties in this suit, and its conclusions and factual findings are highly probative of discrimination.

1. Background....

* * *

Trial judges are busy. The bold synopsis—or any up-front summary—will help the judge by putting the critical information first. That way, the judge does not waste time searching through your document, looking for the point. Judges will appreciate that.

2. Organize overtly.

Now, suppose that the judge has the time to read your whole document. How will the judge differentiate your case, your issues, your points, from all the other cases on the docket? The best way to ensure that a trial judge will understand your case is to make the organization of your paper obvious. Make your organizational plan overt.

Section headings.

To do that, one good technique is to use short, boldface headings for each new section. By using short, boldface headings, you allow the judge, at any point in the text, to refer to a subject heading and quickly know where she is. Headings are cues to large-scale organization. For example:

Motion in Limine

This motion asks the court to exclude evidence that Regional Hospital fired Nurse Esther Green. The firing was a "subsequent remedial measure" and is inadmissible under Rule 407.

1. **Background.** This case was filed on...

2. **Authority.** Under the Federal Rules of Evidence...

3. **Argument.** Evidence of Nurse Green's dismissal is not admissible...

* * *

The busy judge may want to skip ahead to the critical information, and the headings allow that. The busy judge may forget what's going on in your case, and the headings bring the judge's attention back into focus. In short, the headings make it easy on the judge. And that's good.

Enumeration and tabulation.

To cue the judge about the small-scale organization, I recommend that legal writers break up long or complex ideas into smaller chunks of text. Use enumeration (*1, 2, 3* or *a, b, c*) and tabulation (setting off text with hard returns or bullets) to help you organize the text, highlight important material, and cue the judge about the structure of the paragraphs and sentences—the small-scale organization. In other words, these techniques tell the judge where you are with this idea, as opposed to where you are in this document.

Just to clarify what I mean by enumeration and tabulation, here are some examples:

An example of enumeration:

Legal documents should be (1) lettered, (2) numbered, or (3) tabulated.

An example of tabulation:

Legal documents should be

> lettered,
>
> numbered, or
>
> tabulated.

An example of enumeration and tabulation:

Legal documents should be

> 1. lettered,
>
> 2. numbered, or
>
> 3. tabulated.

Even for something as common as reciting of a rule of law, you can use tabulation to present the rule in a clear and direct way:

Instead of this:

> To decide if the limits on selling the plaintiff's car are valid, courts have distinguished between a "direct and total deprivation" of the right to sell, and "mere impingement" of that right. *Spielman-Fond, Inc. v. Hanson's, Inc.*, 379 F. Supp. 997, 999 (D. Ariz. 1973). A direct and total deprivation of the right to sell is more serious. *Id.* It means preventing the sale by seizing the car or by enforcing statutory or contractual terms that prohibit the sale. *Id.* Mere impingement simply means discouraging the sale or making it more difficult. *Id.*

Try this:

> **Rule of Law.** To decide if the limits on selling the plaintiff's car are valid, courts have distinguished between:
>
> 1. a "direct and total deprivation" of the right to sell, and
>
> 2. "mere impingement" of that right.
>
> *Spielman-Fond, Inc. v. Hanson's, Inc.*, 379 F. Supp. 997, 999 (D. Ariz. 1973). A direct and total deprivation of the right to sell is more serious. *Id.* It means preventing the

sale by seizing the car or by enforcing statutory or contractual terms that prohibit the sale. *Id.* Mere impingement simply means discouraging the sale or making it more difficult. *Id.*

With boldface headings, enumeration, and tabulation, the your documents will stand out. Your points will be understandable. Your case will capture the judge's attention.

3. Be honest.

In his excellent book, *Writing to Win: The Legal Writer,* Steven Stark lists "Thirteen Rules of Professionalism in Legal Writing." Here are the first four rules:

1. Never lie, under any circumstance.
2. Don't use euphemisms to disguise the truth.
3. If it's not required, hedging is a form of dishonesty.
4. Avoid the use of hyperbole to distort the truth of your assertions.[7]

Wow. Do you get the impression that Stark, a former judicial clerk and an experienced litigator, is big on honesty? Well trial judges are, too. Consider a quotation on honesty and candor from Judge Stanley Sporkin, formerly of the federal district court in Washington, D.C.

A lawyer's credibility with the judge...is the key to any litigation. Candor is essential. Be honest with the judge....[8]

So in every court paper you submit to a trial judge, be honest.

---

7. Stark, *Writing to Win,* at 269.
8. Stanley Sporkin, *The Inside Scoop,* 27 Litigation 3, 3 (Spring 2001).

Be honest about the facts.

Tell the truth about the facts of your case. Don't omit relevant facts, even if they are unfavorable. Don't fudge. And by fudge, I mean to falsify or fake. If you fudge, you risk your credibility. Remember that several potential audiences can scrutinize your court paper besides your colleagues and your own client: the trial judge, the judge's clerk, and—since most court papers are public documents—the press. Someone will figure out that you've fudged on the truth and bring it to the judge's attention.

And don't forget opposing counsel. One experienced litigator reminded me that in a lawsuit, opposing counsel is getting paid to look for your mistakes: "With a paid critic always checking your work, it just doesn't make sense to fudge."[9]

If you do fudge, you'll lose credibility with the judge, and it might mean sanctions or bar discipline. So write about the facts as favorably as possible for your client, but write honestly.

Be honest about the law.

Sometimes amateurs make mistakes in this area, like the student in this story, who omitted part of the rule of law:

> In the case the students were working on, the rule was that the court should look at five factors to determine the reliability of a witness. Tom chose to discuss only three of the factors and omit the two that hurt his case. [His writing instructor] commented on this problem by writing, "What about the other two factors?" [Tom responded], "Why put them in? They kill my case."[10]

---

9. Kamela Bridges, comments to the author.

10. Anne Enquist, *Critiquing Law Students' Writing: What the Students Say Is Effective*, 2 J. of Leg. Writing Inst. 145, 165 (1996).

That's a naive mistake by a novice legal writer, and I hope it doesn't sound familiar. You can't afford to make that mistake. Read the cases you cite, report their holdings accurately, and check thoroughly to be sure that your cases are still good law.

But why? In Tom's case, the writing instructor had the right response. If you don't report the rule of law accurately, the instructor said, "the State [opposing counsel] will seize on your omission and argue your lack of candor to the court."[11] If you are dishonest about the law, opposing counsel will not let the judge forget it. Judge Sporkin put it this way:

> If you try to spin a court by hiding a key decision that goes against you, the chances are the judge will find out about the decision either from your adversary or from a law clerk. At that point, your credibility is zero.[12]

An up-front summary, an obvious organizational plan, and honesty: three writing skills that will please trial judges—and might even surprise them.

For Affidavits

Most lawyers will need to prepare an affidavit at some time; many will write dozens, if not hundreds. So how effectively are you writing them? For most lawyers, writing an affidavit is strictly routine: drag out an old form, duplicate it, and change the details. Done. The result is a formulaic and bland document. Formulaic and bland is perhaps fine for some affidavits.

But many affidavits are important. You might be counting on an affidavit to get a crucial point across to the opposing counsel, the judge, or the hearing examiner. So how can you make your affidavit stand out from the routine and the mundane?

---

11. *Id.*
12. Stanley Sporkin, *The Inside Scoop*, 27 Litigation 3, 3 (Spring 2001).

If you want people to read and understand your affidavits quickly and easily, you should apply three simple techniques:

1. Use the bold synopsis.

I've said it throughout this book, but I'll say it again: One of the most important principles in legal writing is to provide an up-front summary. Put the critical information first. I'm reiterating it because it is so often ignored. And affidavits, of all legal documents, are among the worst offenders. Usually, the main point an affidavit is buried somewhere in the middle of the document. For example, read this affidavit and pay attention to when you know what the critical point is.

AFFIDAVIT

STATE OF TEXAS   §

                                   §

COUNTY OF TRAVIS   §

DENNIS RAGLEY, being duly sworn, deposes and says:

1. My name is Dennis Ragley. I am over 21 years of age, of sound mind, and I have personal knowledge of the facts stated herein.

2. I am the District Supervisor for ReadyFoods, Inc., and I am responsible for 10 restaurants in the south Texas area, including the Beaumont Freddy's restaurant.

3. On July 10, 1999, I was called by Celia Gonzales, assistant manager at the Beaumont restaurant, and was informed that a shift manager, Kenneth Ivey, had called in and said that he would not work his scheduled shift because his cat had died that morning. In addition, Ivey had not found someone to cover his shift during his absence.

4. I called Kim Henderson, who was originally scheduled to begin working at the restaurant as the General Manager on

July 17, 1999, and asked if she would cover Kenneth Ivey's shift since he had not found anyone to cover his shift.

5. I also asked Kim Henderson to suspend Kenneth Ivey without pay until I could speak with the company's human resources department concerning proper discipline.

6. After speaking with Demetria Suka, the human resource administrator, and Ted Whitney, General Counsel for ReadyFoods, Inc., I decided that Kenneth Ivey should be demoted for failing to work his scheduled shift and for failing to find a person to cover his shift. The fact that Kenneth Ivey was a male had absolutely no bearing on my decision to demote Mr. Ivey.

7. No other employee has ever been given time off for the death of his or her pet.

8. Mr. Ivey was demoted because he had shown by his actions that he could not handle the responsibility of being a shift manager.

9. The foregoing Affidavit consisting of one (1) typewritten page is true and correct.

FURTHER AFFIANT SAYETH NAUGHT

What is the critical information in this affidavit? It is that Mr. Ivey was demoted after he missed work because his cat died. He was not demoted, the affiant asserts, because he is a male. Now, where did you realize that? Probably in paragraph 6; that is where I grasped the main point of the story—the critical information in the affidavit.

But there is no reason an affidavit must be written that way, with the critical point hiding in paragraph 6. Affidavits, like nearly all legal writing, ought to introduce the main point right up front. You can put the main point up front with a bold synopsis.

I suggest that all affidavits contain a bold synopsis. To create a bold synopsis for an affidavit:

- Write a brief synopsis of the main point of the affidavit and identify the affiant.

- Keep the synopsis to 40 or 50 words.
- Put the synopsis up front, indented, and in boldface type.

A bold synopsis for the original affidavit might look like this:

This affidavit, by Kenneth Ivey's supervisor Dennis Ragley, explains that Ivey was demoted because he missed his shift — after his cat had died — and because he did not find someone to cover his shift. Ivey was not demoted because he is a male.

This bold synopsis tells the reader, in a brief and forceful way, the critical point of the affidavit, right up front. Beginning affidavits this way benefits both the writer and the reader.

The writer benefits because creating the bold synopsis makes you think hard about what you're asserting in the affidavit. The bold synopsis helps you to focus your writing on the critical point. It makes you articulate your point, succinctly.

Readers benefit because the bold synopsis allows them to quickly grasp the point of the affidavit even if they do not have time to read the whole thing. But for readers, the bold synopsis is more than just a time-saver. When readers scan the bold synopsis before reading the main text, it becomes easier to follow the story in the affidavit; the story makes sense the first time through. Plus, when the ending is spelled out up front, readers tend to fit the story to the ending — and that's persuasion.

2. Use headings to ease the reader's way.

To make affidavits more readable, easier to follow, and more inviting to the eye, use headings.

- Put headings in boldface type so they stand out.
- Use some topic headings (one or two words each).

- Use some phrasal headings—cogent phrases that preview the factual assertions.

Headings in affidavits can be very effective. They cue the reader about content and organization. They break up long blocks of text. They make documents easier to skim.

Most lawyers know that headings work well in motions, briefs, and agreements. Then why don't lawyers use headings in affidavits? Well, you may be thinking, affidavits are a written form of testimony. No one testifies using subject headings. That's odd.

But no one testifies with paragraph numbers, either, yet nearly all affidavits use them. Let's be clear: an affidavit is not a transcript of testimony—you don't put questions and answers in it. Instead, an affidavit is "a voluntary declaration of facts written down and sworn to by the declarant."[13] It is a prepared statement: written out, thought over, polished. So why can't you use headings in an affidavit?

You can. Here is the original affidavit with headings added:

The affiant.

1. My name is Dennis Ragley. I am over 21 years of age, of sound mind, and I have personal knowledge of the facts stated herein. I am the District Supervisor for ReadyFoods, Inc., and I am responsible for 10 restaurants in the south Texas area, including the Beaumont Freddy's restaurant.

Events surrounding Ivey's demotion.

2. On July 10, 1999, I was contacted by Celia Gonzales, an assistant manager at the Beaumont restaurant, and was informed that a shift manager, Kenneth Ivey, had called the restaurant and said that he would not work his scheduled shift because his cat had died that morning. In addition, Kenneth Ivey had not found someone to cover his shift during his absence.

---

13. *Black's Law Dictionary* 21 (Pocket ed., Bryan A. Garner, ed., West 1996).

3. I called Kim Henderson, who was originally scheduled to begin working at the restaurant as the General Manager on July 17, 1999, and asked if she would cover Kenneth Ivey's shift since he had not found anyone to cover his shift.

4. I also asked Kim Henderson to suspend Kenneth Ivey without pay until I could speak with the company's human resources department concerning proper discipline.

Reasons for Ivey's demotion.

5. After speaking with Demetria Suka, the human resource administrator, and Ted Whitney, General Counsel for ReadyFoods, Inc., I decided that Kenneth Ivey should be demoted for failing to work his scheduled shift and for failing to find a person to cover his shift. The fact that Kenneth Ivey was a male had absolutely no bearing on my decision to demote Mr. Ivey.

6. No other employee has ever been given time-off for the death of his or her pet.

7. Mr. Ivey was demoted because he had shown by his actions that he could not handle the responsibility of being a shift manager.

The addition of headings makes the affidavit easier to understand, easier to follow and more persuasive.

3. Create a neat, clean look by eliminating formulaic clutter.

Too much of what gets passed on from old affidavits to new affidavits is archaic, formulaic clutter. For example, many affidavits begin with a caption like this:

STATE OF TEXAS   §

                               §

COUNTY OF TRAVIS   §

Does this type of caption have a name? Does anyone know why it is there? And, most important, is it required in an affidavit?

My informal survey of several dozen lawyers shows that they do not know what it is called, they are not sure why it is there, and they doubt that it is required. After I surveyed those lawyers, I did my best to find out—through researching on my own—what that caption is. I found nothing. If you are reading this and know what it is, please contact me. Until I know what it is and why it is there, it does not go in my affidavits. And I challenge you to follow me—if you don't know what it is, don't put it in.

Another example, from the end of an affidavit, is the familiar phrase:

> FURTHER AFFIANT SAYETH (or SAITH) NAUGHT (or NOT).

That archaic boilerplate actually does have an explanation. Fortunately, someone has done the research on this one, and he is a reputable source. Bryan Garner, in his *Dictionary of Modern Legal Usage*, tells us that the phrase is from Elizabethan England—the late 1500s—and that English lawyers abandoned it long ago. I suggest that American lawyers in 2002 could well abandon this Elizabethan phrase too. So I agree with Garner's counsel on variations of the "further affiant" phrases:

> The best choice, stylistically speaking, is to use these phrases not.[14]

If we apply the techniques I have suggested here to the original affidavit, we greatly improve it:

- We get an up-front summary.
- We get easy-to-follow headings.
- We get a clutter-free, contemporary document.

Here is how the affidavit looks after applying the three techniques:

---

14. Bryan A. Garner, *A Dictionary of Modern Legal Usage* 378 (2d ed., Oxford. U. Press 1995).

Affidavit

This affidavit, by Kenneth Ivey's supervisor Dennis Ragley, explains that Ivey was demoted because he missed his shift—after his cat had died—and because he did not find someone to cover his shift. Ivey was not demoted because he is a male.

Dennis Ragley, under oath, says:

The affiant.

1. My name is Dennis Ragley. I am over 21 years of age, of sound mind, and I have personal knowledge of the facts stated herein. I am the District Supervisor for ReadyFoods, Inc., and I am responsible for 10 restaurants in the south Texas area, including the Beaumont Freddy's restaurant.

Events surrounding Ivey's demotion.

2. On July 10, 1999, I was contacted by Celia Gonzales, an assistant manager at the Beaumont restaurant, and was informed that a shift manager, Kenneth Ivey, had called the restaurant and said that he would not work his scheduled shift because his cat had died that morning. In addition, Kenneth Ivey had not found someone to cover his shift during his absence.

3. I called Kim Henderson, who was originally scheduled to begin working at the restaurant as the General Manager on July 17, 1999, and asked if she would cover Kenneth Ivey's shift since he had not found anyone to cover his shift.

4. I also asked Kim Henderson to suspend Kenneth Ivey without pay until I could speak with the company's human resources department concerning proper discipline.

Reasons for Ivey's demotion.

5. After speaking with Demetria Suka, the human resource administrator, and Ted Whitney, General Counsel for

ReadyFoods, Inc., I decided that Kenneth Ivey should be demoted for failing to work his scheduled shift and for failing to find a person to cover his shift. The fact that Kenneth Ivey was a male had absolutely no bearing on my decision to demote Mr. Ivey.

6. No other employee has ever been given time-off for the death of his or her pet.

7. Mr. Ivey was demoted because he had shown by his actions that he could not handle the responsibility of being a shift manager.

Signed:

In this revised affidavit, the reader gets a bold-synopsis summary right up front, highlighted headings to guide her through the story, and a clutter-free document that is easy to read and understand. This is an affidavit a judge can use.

Chapter 9

Writing to the Appellate Judge

- *State a well-framed issue up front.*
- *Use transitions and connectors.*
- *Avoid personal attacks.*

Hundreds of books and articles have been written on brief writing, and all of them try to help lawyers do a better job of writing to appellate judges and their staffs. Yet too many appellate briefs are still poor. Here's what judges say:

> A good one [a brief] is essential to appellate advocacy, but it is rare. —Hon. Roger J. Miner, United States Court of Appeals, Second Circuit.[1]

> Perhaps 50 percent of the briefs filed with our court are so one-sided and superficial as to be essentially discarded after an initial skimming. —Hon. Albert Tate, Jr., Supreme Court of Louisiana.[2]

> We simply don't have time to ferret out one bright idea buried in too long a sentence. —Hon. Ruth Bader Ginsburg, United States Supreme Court.[3]

---

1. Roger J. Miner, *Twenty-Five "Dos" for Appellate Brief Writers*, 3 Scribes J. Leg. Writing 21 (1992).

2. Albert Tate, Jr., *The Art of Brief Writing: What a Judge Wants to Read*, 4 Litigation 11, 11 (1978).

3. As quoted in Mark Rust, *Mistakes to Avoid on Appeal*, 74 ABA J. 78, 79 (Sept. 1988).

This chapter offers three simple suggestions that will improve your appellate briefs.

1. State a well-framed issue up front.

In *The Winning Brief*, legal-writing expert Bryan Garner says that "every brief should make its primary point within 90 seconds."[4] Judges agree. For example, Judge Nathan Hecht, of the Texas Supreme Court, has encouraged lawyers to lead with the issue:

> Start in the very first sentence with the problem in this case. Put it right up front. Start early. Don't bury it under a lot of verbiage and preliminaries.[5]

Judges say that they often read the issue statements first—even if they are not up front—to get a sense of the case. So don't make the judge flip through your brief to find the issues. If the judge wants to read the issues first, then make it easy; place the issue statements, prominently, at the beginning of the brief (within the limits of the court's required brief format, of course).

Probably the best way to write an issue statement is by using the "deep issue," an approach advocated by Garner. He says that a well-written issue statement should:

- Consist of separate sentences.
- Contain no more than 75 words.
- Incorporate enough detail to convey a sense of story.
- End with a question mark.
- Appear at the very beginning of a memo, brief, or judicial opinion—not after a statement of facts.

---

4. Bryan A. Garner, *The Winning Brief* 48 (Oxford U. Press 1999).

5. As quoted in Bryan A. Garner, *Judges on Effective Writing: The Importance of Plain Language*, 73 Mich. B.J. 326, 326 (1994).

- Be simple enough that a stranger, preferably even a non-lawyer, can read and understand it.[6]

Take special note of that first bullet. Single-sentence issues statements are dying out. I've been teaching my students to write multiple-sentence issue statements since 1997. Other than tradition, there just isn't anything to commend the single-sentence issue statement, especially those that begin with "whether," like this one. I took it from a legal memo addressing an age-discrimination case.

> Whether an employee who was told he was being fired for failing a physical, and who, after the 180-day deadline for filing an age-discrimination claim with the EEOC had passed, heard talk that the firing was age-based and then one week later saw a memo that demonstrated a discriminatory motive, can toll the time limits so that his filing after seeing the memo will be timely?

Honestly, it's not a grammatical sentence but a fragment that needs three words at the beginning: "The question is…" Plus, it's a single sentence of 67 words—too long and too difficult to grasp on the first reading. And the rule that the question must be stated in a single sentence has forced the writer to pile up several awkward clauses.

So join the contemporary trend toward the multiple-sentence issue statement. Take a look at how effective that approach can be. I've rewritten the age-discrimination issue statement here:

> Employees alleging age discrimination have 180 days to file a claim with the EEOC unless the delay is due to employer deception. John Erickson, 55, was told he was fired for failing a physical, but after 180 days had passed he heard talk that his firing was age-based. A week later he saw a memo

---

6. Bryan A. Garner, *The Deep Issue: A New Approach to Framing Legal Questions*, 5 Scribes J. of Leg. Writing 1, 1 (1994–1995).

showing a discriminatory motive. Can he toll the time limits so that his filing after seeing the memo will be timely?

This example reflects a flexible formula that I recommend for writing issue statements in office memos, which are generally not intended to be persuasive. Start with a sentence that summarizes the relevant rule of law—briefly. Then state the key facts in a condensed way. Finally, pose a legal question that can be answered "yes" or "no."

The deep-issue style can also be used effectively for persuasive appellate briefs. Compare these before-and-after issue statements that are intended to be persuasive:

Traditional

Does Alamo Rent-a-Car have a duty to warn tourists of the risks of high crime in parts of Miami where Dutch tourists Gerrit and Tosca Dieperink visited Miami and rented a car from Alamo, and where they then got lost in Miami and where, while stopped at a gas station to ask for directions, Tosca Dieperink was shot and killed in a robbery attempt?

Contemporary

Gerrit and Tosca Dieperink, Dutch tourists, stopped at a Miami gas station for directions, and Tosca was shot and killed during a robbery attempt as she sat in their Alamo rental car. Gerrit sued Alamo for failing to warn him that there was a high crime risk in parts of Miami. Does Alamo have a duty to warn foreign tourists of high crime areas?

Notice that instead of the "law, facts, question" formula of the objective issue statement, this statement omits a statement of the law and emphasizes facts that are favorable to Gerrit Dieperink.

As you can see, the traditional, single-sentence format used by most brief writers is more difficult to read, more difficult to write, and gets the brief off on stilted footing. If you're going to lead with your issue statement—and you should—write it clearly, directly, and in the contemporary style.

2. Use transitions and connectors.

Your brief, even if it addresses a tedious subject, can be pleasant to read if you lead the judge through it easily and smoothly with plenty of transitions and connectors. To see how this suggestion works, consider these two passages taken from a brief. The first is the original; the second is a revision. Ask yourself which is easier to read and why:

Original

The trial court erred in holding that Alamo had a duty to warn the Dieperinks about driving in Miami. In the absence of a special relationship, no duty exists to warn against the criminal acts of third parties. Car-rental firms are not considered common carriers in Florida. Their relationship with their customers is distinct from that of other common carriers and the "special relationships" recognized by case law.

A duty to warn exists only when the threat is foreseeable and creates an unreasonable risk of harm. The threat to the Dieperinks was not foreseeable because Miami crime rates had recently dropped. The Tampa rental agency could not be expected to know the crime situation in Miami. The lack of foreseeability is further evidenced by the industry practice not to warn tourists about the dangers of driving.

The threat of harm was not unreasonable. The Dieperinks' car was not marked as a rental. Criminals could not use the car to target the Dieperinks as tourists. Tourists do get lost, so by removing the rental designations from the car, Alamo had done the only effective thing it could do to protect its customers.

Revision

    The trial court erred in holding that Alamo had a duty to warn the Dieperinks about driving in Miami. That duty—to warn of the criminal acts of third parties—does not arise in the absence of a special relationship. Here the only special relationship that might have been present is the one recognized by case law for common carriers. But in Florida, car-rental firms are not considered common carriers.

    Without a special relationship, a duty to warn exists only when the threat is foreseeable and creates an unreasonable risk of harm. Here the threat to the Dieperinks was not foreseeable for three reasons.

    First, Miami crime rates had recently dropped. Second, the Tampa rental agency could not be expected to know the crime situation in Miami. Third, industry practice was not to warn tourists about the dangers of driving.

    Not only was the threat unforeseeable, the risk of harm was not unreasonable because the Dieperinks' car was not marked as a rental. So criminals could not use the car to target the Dieperinks as tourists. Of course, tourists do get lost, but by removing the rental designations from the car, Alamo had done the only effective thing it could do to protect its customers.

The revision uses several techniques, and it provides transitions and connectors at the sentence level as well as the paragraph level. Specifically:

- If a sentence uses an important word or phrase, repeat that word or phrase—especially at the beginning of the next sentence—to allow faster recognition that the new sentence builds on the previous: *duty, common carrier,* and *foreseeable.*
- Use demonstrative pronouns, like *that,* to tie a word or phrase to the preceding idea.
- Add single-word transitions that signal a contrast, tell the reader that you're talking about our case, or show that you

are elaborating on the previous point. And opt for shorter, simpler transition words for crisper writing: try *and*, *but*, and *so* instead of *moreover*, *however*, and *consequently*.[7]

- For ideas that have discrete parts, use overt set-ups: "The threat was not foreseeable for three reasons." Then fulfill the expectation by using numbered or ordered sentences: *First*, *Second*, and *Third*.
- Add transition sentences or phrases that connect to the previous idea and set up what is to come: *Not only was the threat unforeseeable* and *Of course.*

These methods may seem simple and obvious. But if so, why are so many briefs weak on transitions and connectors?

Perhaps it's the passage of time: it was way back in seventh grade that you learned how to write transition sentences (and topic sentences, too). Have you forgotten? Or perhaps it's payback: in law school you read a thousand judicial opinions; often they were hard to follow and required a lot of rereading—symptoms of poor transitions and missing connectors. So now that the judges have to read what you write, you're giving what you got.

Maybe. But more likely you're writing under harsh deadlines and you do not have time to polish the brief and add the transitions and connectors. Working under a tight deadline is the rule in law practice, so you can't change that. What to do? Two things.

First, get an early start on at least one project and take the time to read and edit it strictly for transitions and connectors. Pay close attention to flow; ask someone not familiar with the case—preferably a nonlawyer—to read it and point out the bumps and hiccups. Edit accordingly. This first step is really a way of getting some intense practice. You may have time to do it only once or twice, but the more times you go through an edit for transitions and connectors, the more they become second nature. Soon writing with strong transitions won't require the extra time— which you don't have.

---

7. Garner, *The Winning Brief* at 199.

Second, list the techniques you used and the words you added. Keep that list by your computer or near where you write. It is your "transitions and connectors checklist." Glance at it as you write; incorporate the ideas into your text. Soon, you will internalize the use of transitions and connectors to create smoothness and flow in your briefs, and you will spend less time editing for them.

3. Stay away from personal attacks.

If you're angry about your case and outraged at the injustice worked on your client, you have several people to vent on. You can attack the judges—the trial judge who ruled against you or the appellate judge you are addressing—and you can attack the opposing side—the lawyer or the party. But don't.

Attacking judges is a bad idea.

If you're going to attack or criticize a judge, it's usually the trial judge. After all, the trial judge may have ruled against your client and caused this appeal. Now you're angry or frustrated. So why not write bluntly about the trial judge's weaknesses and blunders?

One good reason to use a civil tone is that judges know each other, says Margaret Johns in *Professional Writing for Lawyers*: "The judge reading your appellate brief may have just returned from a camping trip with the judge you are attacking. Your attack on a friend will turn the court against you."[8] And even if they are not friends, judges tend to be protective of their judicial comrades, even those on lower courts.[9]

---

8. Margaret Z. Johns, *Professional Writing for Lawyers* 234 (Carolina Academic Press 1998).

9. Dennis Owens, *Appellate Brief Writing in the Eighth Circuit*, 57 J. Mo. B. 75, 82 (March/April 2001).

And remember that you are appealing the judgment, not the judge.[10] Attacking or criticizing the trial judge is an ineffective technique for showing the flaws in the rulings, the reasoning, or the judgment. Rather, you should "show respect for the lower court," says writing expert Steven Stark, "even while questioning its ruling."[11]

What do judges consider to be attacking or criticizing? Many appellate-brief writers may be surprised to learn that judges have a low threshold. For example, Stark offers this advice from U.S. Court of Appeals Judge John Minor Wisdom:

> Do not say "the district court failed to consider" or anything like it. Treat district judges tenderly.[12]

So follow Judge Wisdom's advice and take it easy. You just won't score points by attacking judges.

Attacking opposing counsel is bad idea.

Nearly every book on appellate-brief writing mentions this advice. Here it is from Myron Moskovitz, an experienced appellate lawyer, in his book *Winning an Appeal*: "Many judges place a high value on professional courtesy, and they can become quite annoyed with an attorney who appears to be wantonly patronizing or demeaning to opposing counsel."[13]

But maybe the best way to drive home the point is to tell you what judges say:

> Next on the list of deadly sins come[s]...personal attacks.
> —Hon. Christine M. Durham, Utah Supreme Court.[14]

---

10. *Id.*

11. Steven D. Stark, *Writing to Win: The Legal Writer* 161 (Main Street Books 1999).

12. *Id.*

13. Myron Moskovitz, *Winning an Appeal*, 39 (3d ed., Michie Butterworth 1995).

14. Christine M. Durham, *View from the Bench: Writing a Winning Appellate Brief*, 10 Utah B.J. 34, 36 (Oct. 1997).

Appellate judges are not helped in their work by criticism of the ethics of the other lawyers in the case. Your criticism diminishes you in the eyes of the judges.—Hon. Robert E. Seiler, Missouri Supreme Court.[15]

[U]nless it is actually material to the issues on appeal, it is usually not a good idea to point out the shortcomings of opposing counsel, since to do so risks arousing skepticism in the judge as to the rest of the brief.—Hon. Alice M. Batchelder, U.S. Court of Appeals, 6th Circuit.[16]

Examples of no-nos...include general allegations that the author's opponent "misstated issues and arguments raised by appellants," "made selective and incomplete statements about the evidence," and "distorted the causation issue." Judges' eyes glaze over as we read that kind of prose.— Hon. Patricia Wald, U.S. Court of Appeals, D.C. Circuit.[17]

So don't risk causing that glaze. Be temperate. Let your well-framed issue statement—right up front—and your lucid, well-connected prose win the case; personal attacks won't.

---

15. Owens, *Appellate Brief Writing in the Eighth Circuit*, 57 J. Mo. B. at 82 (comments of justice Robert E. Seiler of the Missouri Supreme Court).

16. Alice M. Batchelder, *Some Brief Reflections of a Circuit Judge*, 54 Ohio St. L. J. 1453, 1458 (1993).

17. Patricia Wald, *19 Tips from 19 Years on the Appellate Bench*, 1 J. App. Prac. & Process 7, 21–22 (1999).

Chapter 10

Writing to the Consumer

- *Translate jargon.*
- *Target readability.*
- *Test the text on the audience.*

In your legal work, do you ever write for consumers? For example:

- If your client sells a product, have you ever written a safety warning?
- If your client has a website, have you ever written a website disclaimer?
- If your client owns a sports venue, have you ever written a limitation of liability for the tickets?

For those situations and more, the primary audience is consumers. Today, legal writing intended for consumers is everywhere, and lawyers write for consumers frequently. This chapter suggests three key ways to improve legal writing intended for consumers, or *consumer drafting*.

To support the suggestions here, I'll be focusing on this limitation of liability, taken from the back of a baseball ticket and typical of consumer drafting:

THE HOLDER IS ADMITTED ON CONDITION, AND BY USE OF THIS TICKET AGREES, THAT HE WILL NOT TRANSMIT OR AID IN TRANSMITTING ANY DESCRIPTION, ACCOUNT, PICTURE OR REPRODUCTION OF THE BASEBALL GAME OR EXHIBITION TO WHICH THIS TICKET ADMITS HIM. BREACH OF THE

FOREGOING WILL AUTOMATICALLY TERMINATE THIS LICENSE.

THE HOLDER ASSUMES ALL RISK AND DANGERS IN-CIDENTAL TO THE GAME OF BASEBALL INCLUDING SPECIFICALLY (BUT NOT EXCLUSIVELY) THE DAN-GER OF BEING INJURED BY THROWN OR BATTED BALLS AND AGREES THAT THE PARTICIPATING CLUBS, THEIR AGENTS AND PLAYERS ARE NOT LI-ABLE FOR INJURIES RESULTING FROM SUCH CAUSES. THE MANAGEMENT RESERVES THE RIGHT TO RE-VOKE THE LICENSE GRANTED BY THIS TICKET.

I'll call that text the *limitation*, and at the end of this chapter I'll present a complete and radical revision of the limitation. Now, the three suggestions.

1. Translate jargon.

Most consumers are not lawyers (thank goodness). So legal jargon—defined as language that lawyers use to communicate with each other[1]—should not be used in consumer drafting. *License* and *agent* are two examples of legal jargon in the limitation that are acceptable when writing for lawyers but that might be confusing to consumers:

License   Black's Law Dictionary says it's a "revocable permission to commit some act that would otherwise be unlawful."[2] For example, entering a sports stadium—which is private property—without a ticket would be

---

1. Bryan A. Garner, *A Dictionary of Modern Legal Usage* 476 (2d ed., Oxford U. Press 1995).

2. *Black's Law Dictionary* 379 (Pocket ed., Bryan A Garner, ed., West 1996).

unlawful, but the ticket holder has a *license*. Lawyers understand that.

But the nonlegal definition from the Oxford Dictionary and Thesaurus is "a permit from an authority to own or use something."[3] For example, you need a license for a dog, a gun, or a car. That's likely to be the kind of "license" a consumer thinks of.

Agent   Black's says it's "one who is authorized to act for or in place of another."[4] It's a broad term, and lawyers know there is a large body of law developed on agency.

But as used in the limitation, it can be misunderstood. The lawyer who wrote the limitation surely meant to limit the liability of all those who act for the management. But consumers could justifiably assume that *agent* means sports agent—it is, after all, a baseball game—and that would be a narrower limitation of liability.

Eliminate such words or translate them into everyday English. To identify these dual-meaning words, consult David Mellinkoff's *Language of the Law*, in which he lists 29 of them,[5] including

action   the process of doing; but to a lawyer, a lawsuit.

consideration careful thought; but to a lawyer, something of legal value.

service   the act of helping; but to a lawyer, delivery of a summons.

Carefully examine your draft for words that have one meaning to lawyers and a different meaning to consumers—legal jargon. And cut the jargon.

---

3. *Oxford Dictionary & Thesaurus* 864 (American ed., Oxford U. Press 1996)

4. *Black's Pocket Edition* at 23.

5. David Mellinkoff, *The Language of the Law* 11–12 (Little, Brown & Co. 1963).

2. Target readability.

To improve the readability of the text in our limitation, you can rework the limitation from three perspectives.

Type.

First get rid of the ALL-CAPITALS typeface. If you want to draw attention to text, but still have it be inviting and readable, use bold-face for emphasis instead of all-caps. When every letter is uppercase, the text becomes harder to read, according to Robin Williams in her *Non-Designer's Design Book*.[6] Plus, all-capitals typefaces are often interpreted as shouting in print. Don't shout at the consumers who are using your product or attending your event.

Second, carefully balance your type size and the number of characters per line. Generally, type sizes of 6 or 7 points are probably too small for consumer documents, but you may need to use 8- or 9-point type sometimes because of space limitations. If you must use small type, the number of characters per line of text becomes important. Try not to exceed 70 characters (letters and spaces) per line. Break the text into columns if you must, but avoid excessive characters per line because "the reader's eye tends to get lost…in moving from the end of one line to the beginning of the next."[7]

Third, know the difference between serifed and sans-serif typefaces, and choose the type you want. Serifed typefaces have—no surprise—serifs: shorts strokes projecting from the ends of the main strokes. Here are three serifed typefaces:

Bookman

Garamond

---

6. Robin Williams, *The Non-Designer's Design Book: Design and Typographic Principles for the Visual Novice* 18, 109 (Peachpit Press 1994).

7. Garner, *A Dictionary of Modern Legal Usage* at 290.

Times New Roman

Sans-serif typefaces have no serifs, like these:

Arial

Futura

Verdana

For shorter texts, sans-serif typefaces are fine. They will give the text a contemporary and informal feel, thus making the text more inviting. But for longer texts, serifed typefaces will be easier to read[8] and will come across as more formal and professional.

```
And avoid Courier, a nonproportional type-
face that will make your documents look like
they were created on a typewriter.
```

Word and sentence readability.

The guru of readability was Rudolf Flesch. Lawyers who must write for consumers should keep his book, *How to Write Plain English: A Book for Lawyers and Consumers*, on their desks. In his book, Flesch explains his readability formula, an index that rates a text for readability based on word length in syllables and sentence length.[9] On the Flesch scale, zero is "very difficult," and 100 is "very easy." Under his formula, a text must score 65 to be considered good consumer drafting. (Most word processors can calculate the Flesch readability score for you.)

The readability score for our limitation is 35—only a few points better than a typical law review article and well below the threshold for good consumer drafting. Because the score is based on word and sentence length, let's first identify some long words to omit, and then address the sentences. Try to eliminate or change these long words:

---

8. *Id.*

9. Rudolf Flesch, *How to Write Plain English: A Book for lawyers and Consumers* 20–26 (Harper & Row 1979).

automatically

condition

exclusively

exhibition

foregoing

incidental

specifically

terminate

(I am not providing suggested substitutes here, although *event* is a good substitute for *exhibition*. As you'll see, my proposed revision of the limitation eliminated most of these words instead of replacing them.)

Next, consider the sentences. The limitation has 109 words and four sentences, for an average of 27 words per sentence. That's not bad, but the longest sentence (the third one) is 47 words. Remember that in each sentence, you ask readers to hold the information in their heads until they reach the period. So the longer the sentence, the more you ask the readers to hold, and the more difficult it becomes.

But consumer drafting should not be difficult to understand; consumer drafters should not ask too much of consumer readers. Instead, deliver the meaning as easily as possible. It's easy to improve the sentence length in our limitation; just break the longest sentence into two sentences:

> The holder assumes all risk and dangers incidental to the game of baseball including specifically (but not exclusively) the danger of being injured by thrown or batted balls.

> The holder agrees that the participating clubs, their agents and players are not liable for injuries resulting from such causes.

That simple revision alone improves the readability because the average sentence length drops to a respectable 22 words. And merely by dividing one sentence into two and shortening the average sentence length, you raise the readability score to 40.

Using "you."

To write well for the consumer audience, you must use the word *you*. The expert, Flesch, called it "The Indispensable You," and devoted a whole chapter to it.[10] The more you resist the second-person *you*, the more stilted and stuffy your writing will become. You end up using phrases like *the holder,* or you use the masculine pronouns *he* and *him* when you obviously include women.

In the limitation, the use of *you* improves readability greatly; it focuses the reader's attention because it makes the text apply to the reader in a concrete way:

Instead of	Write
The holder assumes	You assume
The holder agrees	You agree

I think that using "you" in consumer drafting is the single most important technique for making the text readable and effective. It has the effect of making the document "speak" to the reader, giving the content immediacy and concreteness. If you must define who "you" is early in the document, that's fine.

In my drafting courses, I always notice a marked improved in student work once they get past the fear of using "you."

3. Test the text on the audience.

To draft effectively for consumers, you must get a draft of your document done early enough to run it by some nonlawyers. You need input from the intended audience. Steven Stark, author of *Writing to Win: The Legal Writer,* says that your writing should pass the *Mc-*

---

10. Flesch, *How to Write Plain English* at 44–50.

Donald's test: "If you were to read the document you're drafting aloud in McDonald's, would people understand what you're saying?"[11]

That is a good standard for consumer drafting. Ideally, you would have a dozen typical consumers read the draft and give you responses. Ask your readers questions like these:

- Could you understand everything in the text?
- What was hard to understand?
- What words sounded like legal jargon?
- How easy was it to read?
- What does it mean?

When you ask your test audience those questions, you are likely to receive some criticism. That may hurt your ego a bit, but if you are determined to have the text understood, you need to be open to honest input from the intended audience.

In fact, I tested both our original limitation and a proposed revision on 20 nonlawyers. It turns out that ten were confused about the meaning of *agent*, though only two were confused about *license*. Over all, 95% preferred the revision to the original.

A possible revision.

Based on the responses from real consumers, and relying on the suggestions offered in this chapter, here is a possible revision of the limitation:

> This ticket admits you to the event listed on the front. By using it, you agree not to broadcast or help broadcast any descriptions or pictures of the event. If you do, you must leave the event.
>
> By using this ticket, you accept the risks of attending a baseball game. For example, you could be hit by thrown or

---

11. Steven D. Stark, *Writing to Win: The Legal Writer* 24 (Main Street Books 1999).

batted balls or injured in other ways. Stadium management, its representatives, the teams, and the players are not responsible for those injuries.

Management may revoke this ticket and remove you from the event.

The revision has 92 words, 13 words per sentence, and scores 65 on the Flesch readability scale—just right for consumer drafting. Of course, this draft is not perfect, and it might not satisfy all lawyers. But it is a good example of how lawyers can improve the way they write for consumers.

Chapter 11

Drafting for the
Transactional Lawyer

• *Seek answers to drafting questions.*

• *Beware of "shall."*

• *Use forms for substance, not style.*

Transactional lawyers are those who practice legal drafting. Let me clarify that I am using the term *drafting* in a narrow and specific way to refer to the writing of "legislation, instruments, or other legal documents that are to be construed by others."[1] I do not use the term *drafting* to refer to the writing of letters, memos, briefs, or court documents. So for purposes of this chapter, "drafted documents are those that set out law or rules, that form a self-contained whole, that are meant to govern conduct, and that lack any writer's voice."[2]

Drafting is a specialized type of legal writing—a field in itself. If you must draft anything that will be read by a transactional lawyer—even if it's just a settlement agreement, a release, or a simple contract—you need to know some basics.

---

1. Bryan A. Garner, *A Dictionary of Modern Legal Usage* 297 (2d ed., Oxford U. Press 1995).

2. Joseph Kimble, *How to Mangle Court Rules and Jury Instructions*, 8 Scribes J. Legal Writing 52 (2002).

1. Seek answers to drafting questions.

Imagine that you are a trial lawyer and that you are preparing for an important hearing on a summary-judgment motion. You know that your success before the judge will depend heavily on an important legal argument. Now imagine that you decide not to look for authority to support that point. Instead, you decide to ask a colleague what he argued the last time he had a similar summary-judgment hearing.

No research; just reliance on what someone argued before. That seems odd.

But perhaps your approach will work. After all, your colleague gives you the argument and tells you that when he used the argument, he prevailed. So you know that this argument works. When you ask him where he got the argument, he tells you that he had asked a more experienced attorney and that she gave him the argument. She, in turn, had gotten the argument from someone else, and so on. In fact, you can trace this legal argument back many years. Thus, the argument is old. But it still works.

Oddly, however, no one has recently researched the argument to find authority to support it. Instead, each lawyer has simply relied on the recommendation of another lawyer who used the argument before. And most of the time the argument has been successful.

Sure, there have been a few minor problems, but the attorneys using the argument have passed that information along to the next lawyer, and they tweaked it to work around the problems. Thus, the argument is a hodgepodge of different lawyers' ideas, expressions, and personal preferences. So it's a complicated and dated argument.

Of course, no serious trial lawyer would practice law that way. If the summary-judgment motion depends on a key legal argument, you would thoroughly research the current law to find support for the argument. You might even write up a report of the research. And if you ever needed the same argument again, you would update the research to be sure that the authority is still good.

You would not rely on an argument without knowing the authority for the argument. You would not rely on an argument that had been passed down without updated legal support from lawyer to lawyer for many years. That's malpractice, isn't it?

Yet that's what legal drafters do all the time:

Steve: Hello Andrea, Steve here. I need to draft a [lease, loan agreement, settlement agreement, release, amendment to bylaws, etc.]. Have you ever done one of those?

Andrea: Yes, I have.

Steve: Would you mind shooting me a copy of your last one so I can see how it's put together?

Andrea: Sure.

In 90% of these situations, Andrea got the form—which she is now passing along—from someone else, who got it from someone else, and so on. Usually, no one in that chain has ever consulted a book on legal drafting to see if the document

- is drafted according to contemporary standards,
- uses correct terminology,
- avoids commons drafting pitfalls, and
- follows recognized drafting conventions and usage.

Steve won't do that kind of research either. Often, he will simply change the names, amounts, and dates—then tweak the terms a bit—and use it.

Why is so much legal drafting done this way? Mostly because many lawyers are not aware of the excellent books and guides on legal drafting that are available today. Nearly any question that arises in a drafting project—from word choice, to format, to substantive coverage—has been thoughtfully addressed by an expert in the field.

I offer three examples of common drafting mistakes that could be easily cleared up if drafters would consult the legal-drafting literature.

The serial comma.

Should you place a comma before the *and* in a series of items? What's the correct style for legal drafting? Though the rule in journalism and literary writing is that you may omit the comma before *and*, the rule for legal drafting is to include the comma, like this:

> The buyer agrees to pay principal, interest, and penalties.

Using the serial comma eliminates possible ambiguity in many circumstances. For example, imagine a loan agreement that contained the following provision:

> A demand under section 7.03 must contain the following parts: statement of the amount, statement of the due date, number of the supporting Agreement section, demand and conclusion, in addition to any supporting attachments.

Must the demand contain separate *demand* and *conclusion* sections, or is the *demand and conclusion* one section? Using the serial comma makes it clear:

> A demand under section 7.03 must contain the following parts: statement of the amount, statement of the due date, number of the supporting Agreement section, demand, and conclusion, in addition to any supporting attachments.

Every contemporary text on legal drafting explains that drafters should use the serial comma before *and*. So don't rely on your best guess or what you read in the newspaper or in another drafted document. Be sure. Look it up.

"Whereas" recitals.

It was once common to begin a contract with an introduction of the parties followed by a series of paragraphs, beginning with the word *whereas*, that explained the background of the transaction. Though it is still acceptable to explain the background of the transaction, it is no longer good drafting practice to use *whereas*. Experts have criticized the word for many years. Here is a comment from Richard Wincor's *Contracts in Plain English*, published in 1976:

> By now it will be clear that no particular form introduced by "Whereas" clauses is necessary in making contracts.[3]

Again, nearly every book on legal drafting has declared that *whereas* clauses are obsolete. If you're still using the word, look it up in a drafting text.

Use of "and/or."

If you read books on legal drafting, you will not a find a more widely condemned phrase than *and/or*:

> The hybrid conjunction and disjunction, "and/or" has caused legal trouble for years. Critics have railed against it, and judges have construed it against lawyers who were foolish enough to persist in using it. — Barbara Child, *Drafting Legal Documents.*[4]

> Since both *and* and *or* are potentially ambiguous, combining them into one term only multiplies the ambiguity. Because of this and the term's total lack of grace, *and/or* has been the subject of considerable judicial abuse. — Thomas R. Haggard, *Legal Drafting in a Nutshell.*[5]

> A legal and business expression dating from the mid-19th century, *and/or* has been vilified for most of its life — and rightly so. — Bryan A. Garner, *A Dictionary of Modern Legal Usage.*[6]

---

3. Richard Wincor, *Contracts in Plain English* 15 (McGraw-Hill 1976).

4. Barbara Child, *Drafting Legal Documents: Principles and Practices* 327–328 (2d. ed., West 1992).

5. Thomas R. Haggard, *Legal Drafting in a Nutshell* 118–119 (West 1996).

6. Garner, *A Dictionary of Modern Legal Usage* at 56.

Some experts say *and/or* is not so bad, like Kenneth Adams, author of *Legal Usage in Drafting Corporate Agreements.* He classifies *and/or* as "one of the more benign drafting evils."[7] But even he admits that he avoids it:

> I try to avoid using *and/or* in my drafting and use instead *X or Y or both,* or, when more than three items are involved, *one or more of A, B, and C.*[8]

So the better practice is to avoid using it at all.

In addition to these three common drafting pitfalls that you would avoid if you consulted drafting sources, here's a short list of other outmoded drafting terms, with comments from the experts:

Herein, therein, hereof, thereof, hereby, thereby, hereinafter, etc.	"[T]otally unnecessary....Any lawyer who thinks such words impress clients is a lawyer who simply does not have a firm grip on reality."*
Said _____	"[Has] been the curse of legal writing as long as there have been lawyers."**
That certain _____	"[B]ureaucratic pomp...best avoided."***
In witness whereof and *Witnesseth*	"[T]he whole mess is easily dispensed with.... It seems to have originated from an early formbook writer's mistake."****

* Haggard, *Legal Drafting in a Nutshell* at 168.

** Robert J. Martineau, *Drafting Legislation and Rules in Plain English* 92 (West 1991).

*** Adams, *Legal Usage in Drafting Corporate Agreements* at 111.

**** Garner, *A Dictionary of Modern Legal Usage* at 938.

---

7. Kenneth A. Adams, *Legal Usage in Drafting Corporate Agreements* 109 (Quorum Books 2001).

8. *Id.* at 110.

So the next time you instinctively use a phrase or word that only a lawyer would use, or anything you're not sure of, consult the experts. You'll set yourself apart from the average drafter.

If you don't have a good drafting text available, then choose any one from the following list; these are the best contemporary drafting texts:

- Barbara Child, *Drafting Legal Documents: Principles and Practices* (2d ed., West 1992).
- Thomas R. Haggard, *Legal Drafting in a Nutshell* (West 1996).
- Robert J. Martineau, *Drafting Legislation and Rules in Plain English* (West 1991).
- Bryan A. Garner, *Guidelines for Drafting and Editing Court Rules* (Admin. Off. of the U.S. Cts. 1996) (reprinted in 169 F.R.D. 176).
- Kenneth A. Adams, *Legal Usage in Drafting Corporate Agreements* (Quorum Books 2001).
- Peter Butt & Richard Castle, *Modern Legal Drafting: A Guide to Using Clearer Language* (Cambridge Univ. Press 2001) (written from a British perspective).

These are the places to find answers to drafting questions. Do not guess. Do not rely on half-remembered principles from law school, where most lawyers got no training in legal drafting. Do not rely on old forms passed on by colleagues. If you have a legal-drafting question, look it up.

2. Beware of "shall."

Did you know that *shall* is the most misused of all words in legal drafting?[9] It may be conventional wisdom that *shall* imposes an

---

9. Joseph Kimble, *The Many Misuses of "Shall,"* 3 Scribes J. Legal Writing 61, 61 (1992).

obligation, but well-read drafters know that it is fraught with problems. Here's what the experts say about *shall*:

> Drafters use it mindlessly. Courts read it any which way.—Joseph Kimble, *The Many Misuses of "Shall."*[10]

> Lawyers misuse it. They confuse the imperative *shall* with the future tense and fail to distinguish between the various senses of *shall* in their documents.—Michèle M. Asprey, *"Shall" Must Go.*[11]

> [O]ne of the reasons *shall* is in such disrepute is that drafters use it for too many...purposes.—Thomas R. Haggard, *Legal Drafting in a Nutshell.*[12]

Surprised? Don't be embarrassed if you're an experienced drafter and you were not aware of the problems with *shall*. Most lawyers aren't. But take a moment to look up *shall* in *Words and Phrases*, and you'll see why it's a problem. It gets litigated a lot. That's a bad thing by itself. Why use a word that you know invites litigation?

It's litigated a lot because it is often ambiguous. Courts have construed it to mean "absolutely must," or "should," or "may."[13] So the commonly held idea among lawyers that it's an "imperative" word is shaky. Its traditional legal sense is indeed imperative, but its traditional, nonlegal usage was to express future tense in the first person: "I shall die someday."[14] Between the two different meanings and careless use by drafters, the word has lost its efficacy.

Plus, it's archaic. Who uses it? No one—least of all someone in the United States today—except legal drafters. And, as I've said, even legal drafters use it incorrectly much of the time. Given those concerns, there are two possible choices for the lawyer who must draft in a transactional practice.

---

10. *Id.* at 71.

11. Michèle M. Asprey, *"Shall" Must Go*, 3 Scribes J. Legal Writing 79, 79 (1992).

12. Haggard, *Legal Drafting in a Nutshell* at 232.

13. Kimble, *The Many Misuses of "Shall,"* 3 Scribes J. Legal Writing at 75.

14. *Id.* at 62.

The first option is to use *shall* only to impose an obligation or duty on an actor (a person or entity that can perform duties) in the sentence. When used in this way, *shall* means "has a duty to." You can substitute that phrase for *shall* to test whether you have used *shall* correctly; if you have, the sentence will still make sense. This is a simplistic approach, but it works. For example, read these sentences from a child-support order, and notice which one does not work:

1. The Respondent **shall** pay 26% of his monthly net income to the Petitioner as child support.
2. Beginning in the year 2000, 26% of all bonus checks **shall** be paid to Petitioner.

Sentence 1 uses *shall* correctly; sentence 2 does not.

In sentence 1, *shall* imposes a duty on an actor in the sentence: the Respondent (a human being who can perform a duty) shall pay—has a duty to pay—26% of his income to the Petitioner. But in sentence 2, the duty to pay is strangely imposed on the bonus checks. The bonus checks shall be paid—have a duty to be paid—to the Petitioner. Is that what the drafter intended? Certainly not. We know what was intended, but the construction is strained. The drafter should have written this: "the Respondent shall pay 26% of his bonus checks to the Petitioner."

This example shows the correct—and incorrect—way to use *shall* to impose a duty. Of course, the problem in sentence 2 is not only with the incorrect use of *shall*; there is also a passive-voice construction: *shall be paid*. But the sentence highlights how drafters make mistakes when using *shall*.

The second option for legal drafters is to avoid *shall* entirely. Some experts recommend this approach. Bryan Garner advises lawyers to "delete every *shall*"[15]; and Michèle Asprey, a plain-language expert from Australia, wrote an article called *Shall Must Go*.[16]

---

15. Bryan A. Garner, *Legal Writing in Plain English: A Text with Exercises* 105 (U. Chicago Press 2001).

16. Asprey, *"Shall" Must Go*, 3 Scribes J. Legal Writing at 79.

It's also the approach I recommend unless you are ready to undertake a thorough study of the word. (By the way, if you do want to study the word, you should read the section on "Creating Legal Consequences" in Thomas Haggard's *Legal Drafting in a Nutshell*[17] and Joe Kimble's article *The Many Misuses of "Shall."*[18])

If you're going to abandon *shall,* try *must* to impose duties and *will* to show agreement or promise (as in a contract).[19]

3. Use forms for substance, not style.

For almost any drafting project, you can find a form document to use as a guide. Some lawyers call these "precedents." Generally, you will have access to two kinds of forms: commercially-produced forms published in books or online, and forms you get from a colleague.

The advice for using forms is simple: *use forms for the substance of the law, not for legal-drafting style.* And even for substance, double-check with another book or an experienced drafter, or both. In formbooks, you may find checklists spelling out the legal requirements for the document you are drafting. Or you may create your own checklist of important substantive content by relying on formbooks. But the drafting style of the forms in nearly all formbooks is poor by contemporary standards.[20] Formbooks are weak on drafting style for two main reasons.

The first reason that formbooks are weak on drafting style is that most formbooks rely on older formbooks, which relied on earlier formbooks, which relied on previous forms, and so on. Thus you might find drafting language in a contemporary form book, published in the 1990s, that reflects the drafting practices of 50 or 100

---

17. Haggard, *Legal Drafting in a Nutshell* at 231–238.
18. Kimble, *The Many Misuses of "Shall,"* 3 Scribes J. Legal Writing at 61.
19. Garner, *Legal Writing in Plain English* at 106.
20. Haggard, *Legal Drafting in a Nutshell* at 67.

years ago. In fact, some formbooks contain language that hearkens back to Victorian England or earlier.[21] Many of these archaic forms were created, not by lawyers, but by clerks who were more interested in sounding erudite than in drafting clearly.[22]

For example, I recently purchased a legal-forms text, published in 1999, whose authors are experienced lawyers. Yet in reviewing the forms, I noticed that they contain all of the following:

- Use of *whereas* clauses.
- Many incorrect uses of *shall*.
- Consistent omission of the serial comma.
- Heavy use of here- and there-words like *herein, hereby,* and *thereof.*
- Repeated use of archaic phrases like *in witness whereof,* and *witnesseth.*

Plus, these forms contain excessive use of the passive-voice, long sentences, and awkward typefaces. These weak drafting practices will surely be continued by users of the book. Bad drafting perpetuates bad drafting.

The second reason formbooks are weak on drafting style is that most commercial formbooks are produced by experts in the substantive field the forms cover, without input from experts in drafting style. It makes sense, of course, to have experts in corporate transactions create corporate-transaction forms. No one would suggest that you can draft effectively without a detailed knowledge of the law. But writing experts can play an important role in preparing forms, too. Unfortunately, those who draft documents and those who create formbooks rarely consult legal-drafting experts. And legal academia has only just begun to recognize and reward expertise in legal drafting.

---

21. Peter Butt & Richard Castle, *Modern Legal Drafting: A Guide to Using Clearer Language* 10, 65 (Cambridge U. Press 2001).

22. David Mellinkoff, *The Language of the Law* 195 (Little, Brown & Co. 1963).

As a result, formbooks generally do not reflect contemporary wisdom in legal drafting. Granted, a form can help you identify the right issues, but it won't help much for how to phrase the draft.[23] So avoid blindly following the language and wording of forms.

---

23. Bryan A. Garner, *The Redbook: A Manual on Legal Style* § 20.3(e) (West Group 2002).

Chapter 12

Writing for the Citizen

- *Format for easy reading.*
- *Shun legalisms and formality.*
- *Use short sentences.*

In your practice, do you ever need to write for the typical citizens—the real people who need to read and understand the rules that apply to them? That kind of writing is usually legislative and regulatory drafting, a narrow specialty within legal drafting. Most lawyers probably assume they never need to write for the citizen. But ask yourself:

- Have you ever written or revised the bylaws for an organization? (When I volunteered to serve in my neighborhood association, that is the first thing they asked me to do.)
- Have you ever needed to draft public rules? (I was once asked to revise the rules for using the local cable-access channel.)
- Have you ever needed to draft a declaration that the parties understand their rights and obligations?

In all of those situations you are writing for the audience of "citizens." So you need to understand that audience and adapt to its abilities, expectations, and needs. For example, most citizens are not lawyers, and many will not be highly educated. How will you write effectively for them? This chapter presents three simple suggestions to improve legal writing intended for citizens.

First, read this legislatively enacted "statement on alternative dispute resolution," taken from the Texas Family Code:

I AM AWARE THAT IT IS THE POLICY OF THE STATE
OF TEXAS TO PROMOTE THE AMICABLE AND NON-

JUDICIAL SETTLEMENT OF DISPUTES INVOLVING CHILDREN AND FAMILIES. I AM AWARE OF ALTERNATIVE DISPUTE RESOLUTION METHODS, INCLUDING MEDIATION. WHILE I RECOGNIZE THAT ALTERNATIVE DISPUTE RESOLUTION IS AN ALTERNATIVE TO AND NOT A SUBSTITUTE FOR A TRIAL AND THAT THIS CASE MAY BE TRIED IF IT IS NOT SETTLED, I REPRESENT TO THE COURT THAT I WILL ATTEMPT IN GOOD FAITH TO RESOLVE BEFORE FINAL TRIAL CONTESTED ISSUES IN THIS CASE BY ALTERNATIVE DISPUTE RESOLUTION WITHOUT THE NECESSITY OF COURT INTERVENTION.[1]

This statement must be included in the first pleading filed by each party in suits affecting the parent-child relationship and in divorce suits.[2] The statement "must be prominently displayed in boldfaced type or capital letters or be underlined and be signed by the party."[3]

I'll call that text the *statement*, and I'll offer my three suggestions in the context of that statement. Afterward I'll present a complete revision of the statement. Now, the three suggestions.

1. Format for easy reading.

When writing for the citizen audience, remember that the format of the text is critical. The visual presentation can make the text either inviting or intimidating. Keep in mind these formatting suggestions:

Use a readable typeface.

The first thing to change is obvious, and I've said it before: change the ALL-CAPS to boldface type. That is, after all, the first

---

1. Tex. Fam. Code Ann. § 102.0085(a) (Vernon Supp. 2002).
2. *Id.* Tex. Fam. Code Ann. § 6.404(a) (Vernon Supp. 2002).
3. Tex. Fam. Code Ann. § 102.0085(b), § 6.404(b) (Vernon Supp. 2002).

option listed in the statute. If you want to draw extra attention to the language, you can put a box around it.

Break up long blocks of text.

The original statement is a solid block of unbroken text. Even after converting it to regular type, it can be off-putting:

> I am aware that it is the policy of the State of Texas to promote the amicable and nonjudicial settlement of disputes involving children and families. I am aware of alternative dispute resolution methods, including mediation. While I recognize that alternative dispute resolution is an alternative to and not a substitute for a trial and that this case may be tried if it is not settled, I represent to the court that I will attempt in good faith to resolve before final trial contested issues in this case by alternative dispute resolution without the necessity of court intervention.

So lawyers writing for citizens should use numbering and white space to break up this block of text and make it more accessible. After all, this statement is important—the citizen readers need to be able to understand it, so help them by formatting it in digestible chunks. Try this:

1. I am aware of

    (a) the policy of the State of Texas to promote the amicable and nonjudicial settlement of disputes involving children and families, and

    (b) alternative dispute resolution methods, including mediation.

2. While I recognize that alternative dispute resolution is an alternative to and not a substitute for a trial and that this case may be tried if it is not settled, I represent to the court that I will attempt in good faith to resolve before final trial contested issues in this case by alternative dis-

pute resolution without the necessity of court intervention.

We may need further textual revisions to make this new format work well, but even as it is, the text is more inviting, simpler to read, and easier to understand.

2. Avoid legalisms and formality.

Legalisms and formalisms are the old, stuffy, fancy words and phrases that characterize legal writing. Not only do they distract and confuse the citizen reader, they often cause unwarranted intimidation. This statement should bring about comprehension, not intimidation. So when you are writing for the citizen audience, mercilessly weed out legalisms and formalisms.

The original statement is full of legalisms and formalisms. For example:

Replace these words and phrases	With these words and phrases
I am aware	I know
amicable	peaceful
non-judicial settlement	out-of-court settlement
alternative dispute resolution	non-court solution
represent	promise
contested issue	dispute (or case)
court intervention	court action

If you carefully scrutinize your drafts for legalistic and unnecessarily formal words, you'll produce a clearer and more understandable text.

3. Use short sentences.

The original statement is 98 words long and has three sentences—for an average sentence length of 33 words. Consumer-drafting expert Rudolf Flesch says that lawyers ought to strive for an average sentence length of 20 words.[4] At 33 words per sentence, this statement has room for improvement.

Plus, the longest sentence in the statement—the third one—is 62 words. That is too long for the citizen audience. Even though an occasional sentence of 40 or 50 words can be manageable, once a sentence goes over 50 words, it becomes difficult to follow.

And please remember that "difficult to follow" is a relative term. We lawyers are used to long sentences; we began reading them in our casebooks in law school. But for the typical citizen, the statement's average sentence length, and the third sentence in particular, are more difficult than necessary.

To improve sentence length and readability, simply break the third sentence into two, like this:

> I recognize that alternative dispute resolution is an alternative to and not a substitute for a trial and that this case may be tried if it is not settled.

> I represent to the court that I will attempt in good faith to resolve before final trial contested issues in this case by alternative dispute resolution without the necessity of court intervention.

That simple revision improves readability by decreasing the average sentence length to 25 words. But we can do more. Next, consider a full revision of the statement.

---

4. Rudolf Flesch, *How to Write Plain English: A Book for Lawyers and Consumers* 24 (Harper & Row 1979).

The revision.

Based on the suggestions in this chapter, and after testing some drafts on typical citizens, I wrote this revision of the statement:

> **By signing this statement, I affirm that:**
>
> **1. I know that Texas promotes peaceful, out-of-court settlements of family-law cases.**
>
> **2. I know about non-court solutions, including mediation.**
>
> **3. I know that non-court solutions are an option and not a substitute for a trial.**
>
> **4. I know that this case may go to court if it is not settled.**
>
> **5. I promise to try—in good faith—to resolve this case out of court.**

In this revision, there are 71 words, with an average sentence length of 12 words. The readability is greatly improved. But some lawyers will doubtless have concerns. Let me address two.

First, I eliminated the phrase *alternative dispute resolution.* Most lawyers know what it means, but most typical citizens do not. (Try asking a nonlawyer.) To work around that phrase, I used variations of the phrase *settle out of court.*

Second, to some lawyers, the phrase *settle out of court* is redundant because all settling is "out of court." But in my survey of 50 typical, nonlawyer citizens, more than half thought *settle* meant **any** resolution—even when the judge resolved the dispute. Only *settle out of court* clearly conveyed the meaning that the settlement was without the judge's involvement. Thus, *settle out of court* conveyed the desired meaning more clearly.

Perhaps some lawyers and legislators will not want to go this far in revising the statement. That is not surprising; most lawyers will have different comfort levels with the tone and format of legal writing that is intended for citizens. But what is surprising is how often we lawyers forget our audience. This revision is just one example of how lawyers can improve the way they write for citizens.

Chapter 13

Conclusion

Who is my audience?

You should answer that question first on any legal-writing project. I hope this book has prompted you to think about audience every time because the measure of good writing is whether the audience gets the message. It doesn't matter if your document looks or sounds "legal." What matters is that it conveys the legal meaning to the intended audience. To me, the only good legal writing is audience-focused writing. I hope you agree.

I also hope that you detected the major themes in this book—the broad principles that drive audience-focused writing. Mainly there are three:

- *Write naturally.* Good legal writing is smooth, readable, and natural. It's not overly formal, esoteric, or pompous.
- *Make information accessible.* The most important information should be up front in legal writing. Other information should be well organized and clearly signposted.
- *Consult the authorities.* When you have questions about writing, don't guess. Look things up. That's what professional writers do.

If you target your audience and remember these principles, your legal writing will be a cut above the ordinary.

Index